Introduction

You are being bullied at work, or someone you know and care for is being bullied at work. You wish you knew what to do to make it stop? As a going-in proposition with regards to workplace bullies, I will tell you that my belief is that the workplace bully (as a workplace oppressor) is a coward. The workplace bully is a person who bargains for his self-worth by devaluing you and me, rather than improving or resolving conflict in himself. With this philosophical perspective, this handbook is full of practical tactics to stop the bully at work from destroying you and those around you.

- Currently Bullied – 7%
- Been Bullied – 20%
- Witnessed Bullying – 21%
- Aware of Bullying – 23%
- Unaware of Bullying – 28%

Everyone desires to work in, and lead in a bully-free workplace. However not everyone knows how to stop the bully from destroying their work life, or how to create and promote a bully-free culture in their workplace. If you are reading this handbook you are already on the path to gaining the skills to (1) stop the bully, and (2) promote and achieve a bully-free workplace, so congratulations! This handbook is field tested and will show you how to confront the bully in a safe manner, and begin promote a bully-free culture in your workplace.

This Stop-The-Bully handbook has twelve sections, including a review of contemporary literature regarding bullying, a review of the language associated with the bully phenomenon, an examination of bullying within the contemporary workplace and the steps you must take to stop the bully. I also offer an insight to the significance of anti-bullying behavior to contemporary leaders, and what you as a leader need to know on a personal level to eliminate bullying behavior from your workplace and institute positive behavior as a cultural norm

Contents

<u>Did You Like This Hand Book?</u>

<u>Notes</u>

Section I: Who Am I and Why Should You Believe Me?

I have been an employee in organizations where bullies have prevailed. I now know what a bully is. I will tell you that bullies come in all forms, as customers, bosses, as colleagues and even as subordinates. I know from experience as a leader and an employee that an encounter with a bully is destructive, both personally and professionally. The insidious nature of bullying attacks at the core of each individual, and at the heart of an organization and destroys the will to produce and to serve. I have studied deviant workplace behaviors at length, and the academic literature is rich in detail about the antecedence and consequences of bullying in the workplace. As an experienced leader and manager, as well as a certified Executive Leadership Coach, my goal is now to help you to stop the bully in your workplace, and to manifest you're highest and most joyful work life. My unique gift is helping you begin the journey; whether you are a target or observer of bullying, or leader and manager desiring to overcome workplace challenges, I will intentionally and thoughtfully help you to change your emotional state while challenging your common understanding of workplace bullying.

We have all met the bully at some point in our career and the important question is whether we all have the skills to effectively stop the bully, or to create an alternative reality? I am most fortunate to have completed a very successful professional career as a federal leader, where I have met the bully and survived. Along the way I have participated in a variety of professional leadership programs (Harvard, Brookings, Federal Executive Institute, Center for Creative Leadership, and the FBI Academy). I can now share my knowledge and insights about the bully in your workplace, I will help you to shift from enduring bullying behavior towards achieving the ability to say stop! You will begin to return to your happy work life again, and begin to feel renewed, empowered, and confident about your ability to stop your bully.

What differentiates me as an author on bullying, incivility and other deviant workplace behaviors is my street credibility! As both a leadership practitioner and academic sleuth I have been working in, coaching in, teaching in, mentoring in, and learning about the workplace for the past 30 years. While I recognize that as a former federal executive it is uncool to acknowledge that I too have experienced bullying first hand, I believe the first step in stopping the cycle of bullying is to be honest. I therefore will restate as a survivor of workplace bullying that I have also experienced and observed bullying behaviors directed towards me and around me, from supervisors, colleagues and subordinates. Through my personal and professional experience I can relate to what you are enduring, and how you feel about bullying in the workplace.

My instructional strategy within this handbook includes the telling of stories and showcasing bullying behavior (within the various stories the names are changed to protect the innocent and many aspects are embellished to illuminate a teaching point). By exploring the antecedence and consequences of bullying, I will help you move forward with tangible actions designed to secure immediate results. You will learn to say stop to your bully and he will hear you!

If we choose to trade our time for money then I propose that our work life should be fulfilling and joyful, and free from physical, mental and emotional harm.   As an organizational observer and practitioner, I will show you how to address your bully from both a sound theoretical and practitioner perspective. The simplicity of my strategy focuses on creating and managing positive behaviors through telling stories and answering questions.

In order to create a deeper understanding of bully behavior, I offer you some contemporary perspective about bullying literature in general, thus the handbook on stopping your workplace bully starts with an overview of literature to help prepare you for the tactical steps outlined in the last sections of the handbook.

Section 2: Bullying Research And Literature And Why It Became Important To Us.

>
>
> *Roger is all business, that's just the way he is.   He thinks he doesn't mean any harm, but he can get very snippy with other people on the team. He makes the company a ton of money and his customers love him.   He brought a whole lot of his old customers with him when he came to us, and we are afraid that he will take them elsewhere if we lost him.   Yes, he can be a jerk.   Yes he made the ladies in the back office cry again last week. Yes, he did poke fun at the cleaning crew.   Yes, he does demand a lot more of my time and attention than any other employee, but he brings in more revenue than anyone else.   Yes, I know three of my top-level guys have left since he came on board, which is all the more reason why I cannot afford to get lose him.   Yes, he can be sarcastic and inattentive during my staff meetings. OMG I must be wasting his time. Crap! Yes, I am an idiot….. This guy is a bully and has to go and I owe the entire team an apology and a get-well-strategy ASAP!*

Warning - if you don't like theoretical information you can ignore this section. But for some learners I find that theory helps them to understand the present phenomenon being explored, and I personally believe it is difficult to plan strategy for the future without understanding some of the theory. This section is specifically written for them.

Power

As a foundational aspect of any relationship, the sharing of power is significant, especially in the workplace where relationships are embodied within role-based expectations which guide employee behavior. The traditional workplace dynamic of giving, taking, and experiencing powerfulness is described as the phenomenon of empowerment. Contemporary literature has focused on how leaders can share their power in order to create situational empowerment. Although power can also be understood as a "have or have not" scheme where role-based power is supported by an organizational structure or system, everyone in the organization holds a certain amount of power (even those who are bullied). Empowerment is the sharing of power in a relationship with another person, and it requires assistance from both parties. While a leader can't make an employee powerful just by bestowing power upon him, because the employee must act on that power to make it true. Similarly a leader can't take away all the power an employee has, without the employee allowing it. When people in the workplace (and victims of bullying) allow their power to be given or taken away, they will experience loss of motivation, a loss of effort, and finally the experience of helplessness. Mary Parker Follett (1918) was an American social worker, management consultant and pioneer in the fields of organizational theory and organizational behavior. She was one of two great women management gurus in the early days of classical management theory, and she advocated for a reciprocal leadership approach whereby the leader guides the group and is at the same time guided by the group, in a partnership of distributed power that is interactive and shared.

Work Engagement

The economic demands on today's workplace drives organizations to search for solutions to remain productive and profitable (Jacobs, 2013). A solution appears to be getting employees more engaged in their work, to include achieving a better understanding about why employees are not fully engaged in their workplace.

> *Story #2.   The Value Of Discretionary Contribution*
>
> *Jamie was a champion worker, skilled in his trade, engaged in the workplace and self-motivated. He neither sought out nor accepted praise, and for Jamie, his performance and output was a personal matter. Every organization should have 1000 Jamie's on their team, for then there would be peace in the land and all would prosper. Jamie was the first person to acquaint me with the notion of 'discretionary-contribution': for Jamie worked as effectively and as efficiently as he did because he loved his*

Employees who are engaged in their work are more likely to go above and beyond the duties that are expected of them and perform tasks that are helpful to colleagues, and to the organization at large. Employee engagement refers to the positive, fulfilling, motivational state of mind that workers encounter when they are completely immersed in their work to the point that time flies by. Engaged employees are enthusiastic and have an affective and energetic connection to their work, as opposed to finding their work stressful and demanding.

Bullying has a negative impact upon employee engagement in the workplace. Personal and emotional safety are antecedents to worker engagement, and psychological perceptions of safety are the most significant. Psychological safety, refers to the feeling of being "able to show and employ one's self without fear of negative consequence to self-image, status, or career" (Kahn, 1990). Employees are more likely to become engaged in their work when they feel psychologically safe in their professional surroundings, such that they can let their guard down and perform at their highest and best selves. Noticeably, employees' relationships with their supervisors plays a significant part in determining their level of felt psychological safety. If supervisors are supportive, employees are more likely to relax, be themselves, and say or do what is on their mind. Conversely, when supervisors are not supportive, or are abusive and hostile and exhibit bullying behavior, then employees withhold engagement.

Employees that are fully present in their jobs are more likely to be engaged in positive relationships with coworkers and often bridge gaps between workers of different gender, race, ethnic, and ethical standards.   Both positive and negative engagement are known to be contagious among workers. According to the theoretical concept of emotional contagion, positive and negative experiences can be transferred from one person to another and studies have confirmed that engagement can be transferred between individuals and teams. Accordingly, the presence of one engaged worker makes it probable that there will be several engaged workers in the corresponding workplace, and conversely one unengaged worker will impact other workers.

Psychological safety among workers is experienced as feeling able to employ and show one's self without fear of negative consequences to status, career, or self-image. It is determined by elements of the organization that create non-threatening, predictable, and consistent environments in which workers can engage. A workplace culture that promotes open communication, which is supportive and trusting, and allows employees to feel as though they belong and can be themselves will be more likely to foster feelings of psychological safety. Individual characteristics also play a part in one's level of psychological safety. Individuals tend to be more or less likely to let their guard down on the basis of their level of such personality characteristics such as extraversion, neuroticism, and self-consciousness.

Shame

The experience of shame is negatively-related to innovative behavior. Research has shown us that shame is a powerful negative force with many negative consequences, such as psychopathology, depression, impeded physical health, alcoholism and drug use. It is expected then that shame too may have negative consequences for organizations and that enhancing our knowledge of the consequences of experiencing shame in the work environment has the potential to further our understanding of this under-researched and yet powerful affective force (Duff, 2013).

Story #3.   Marjorie And The Intern's Shame

Marjorie was running late for her meeting with her boss, and while she is typically harsh and demanding of those within her hierarchy, she did not consider herself a bully. Marjorie's level of self-awareness was limited, as she saw her professional success arising out of her ability to isolated personal niceness from demanding output from her employees. Marjory believed that she did not need to be nice to her team - being nice was not what got her promoted into this job. Jim was a new hire… a new intern… that Marjorie had enticed to join the organization and her team. He was young and inexperienced but he had excellent academic credentials and pedigree, as Marjorie knew he was a military brat and the son of a successful Army Officer. On the morning that Marjorie was rushing to her next meeting, which was with her own boss, Jim unfortunately decided to attempt to engage Marjorie in conversation.

Marjorie cut Jim off mid-sentence as he began telling her about his new idea for organizing the vendors' display tables. Marjorie was characteristically rude and discourteous, however because Jim was a new hire he had not been exposed to this side of her personality before. Regardless of Marjorie's' lack of awareness of her inappropriate behavior, Jim recoiled in response to Marjorie's curtness, and he blushed in shame. Jim had not experienced being dismissed before in this manner and he felt instantly demeaned and ashamed. The shame did not arise from what he had done, rather from being humiliated by someone, who up until

*that point he had admired.   As a new employee Jim was experiencing great
uncertainty about his role in the organization, and today was the first time
he had the confidence to offer an innovative insight about the upcoming
tradeshow. And so .... Marjorie never knew the effect of her rude and
discourteous behavior had on the new hire, and Jim in turn withdrew from
engaging with Marjorie and refrained from offering further innovations or
process improvements. Over time, the inevitable outcome was that
Marjorie believed she had made a mistake in hiring Jim, while Jim felt the
same about the job he was hired into. Eventually Jim exercised his
prerogative and commenced the process to seek a new assignment with
another company.*

We understand how psychological withdrawal as a result of shame, the negative form of engagement, impacts innovative behavior, and contemporary organizations embrace innovative behavior as a competitive advantage. Research in the domain of psychology and social psychology suggests that workers typically respond to shame in four ways; avoidance, attack others, attack self, and withdrawal. An avoidance-response is essentially the denial of either the shame-inducing event or experiencing the shame emotion. An attack-others response is an act of verbal or physical aggression towards others. An attack-self response is the engagement in negative rumination about oneself, typically in the form of self-contempt for failing to live up to one's internalized standards, and a withdrawal response can be either a physical or psychological removal of oneself in order to limit additional negative affect stemming from interaction with others.

Recognizing that the essence of innovative behavior is openness to risk taking and withdrawal is a risk adverse behavior, the extent to which shame enacts withdrawal is understood to compromise innovative behavior. Organizations that need employees to engage in innovative behavior, either by implementing more effective ways of doing their work or developing new products and services, may realize operational benefits by controlling the extent to which people experience shame at work. Bullying can be a source of shame for an employee. Bullying that manifests itself in the form of personal insults, uninvited physical contacts such as the status demeaning back slap, rude interruptions, eye rolling and dirty looks, or treating a person as if they are invisible is shameful and shame inducing.

Hames (2013) suggests that we are emerging from an era of workplace crises which in turn speaks to the narrative of weak organizational culture. The world is now focused on the actions of individual leaders and the organizational cultures they cultivate. We are especially interested in understanding cultures that reflect low-trust and high-fear environments, which fail to flourish and ultimately become just another dysfunctional and failing business.   The role of leadership in enabling a healthy culture is then paramount to long-term health of any organization. The question however is, does leadership demonstrate the espoused values as published in the mission and vision statements. Stated another way, how does bullying and other deviant workplace behavior manifest itself in a culture that espouses the respect and dignity of all employees. For leaders to be successful in transforming and building healthy ethical cultures they must first recognize the importance of leading in a manner that embodies a positive culture ambassador.   They must lead their organizations in a perceptible manner, making themselves available, and accessible through informal dialogue, establishing behavioral expectations around values-based decision making and modeling positive behavior.

Rouse (2013) reported that in 2007, the Workplace Bullying Institute (WBI) and Zogby International conducted a nationwide phone survey and found that 37% of respondents reported having been victimized by bullies at work. From these results, the Zogby Institute estimated that roughly 54 million U.S. workers had been targets of workplace bullying. There may be reasons why bullying has not received the kind of attention that it deserves, primarily because there are no federal laws specifically designed to prevent workplace bullying.   A second factor, which contributes to the underreporting of bullying, is that organizational bullies most often hold higher-status positions, and there is some evidence that managers facilitate or tacitly condone bullies because of their perceived productivity, and likeminded supervisors resonate with the more aggressive personality types. A third factor, which illustrates the rise in lateral bullying, is weak management, which facilitates employees of approximately equal rank engaging in deviant workplace behavior and bullying. The fourth and perhaps most insidious factor which contributes to bullying in the workplace is the personalities of the targets of bullies. Targets of bullying often ignore the problem in the beginning stages, they typically have less real or perceived power in an organization and are therefore less likely to report abuse, and they tend to be newer employees and are more likely to be female. Understandably, bullies do not self-identify with the title and view their aggression as justified, as they enjoy higher social standing than targets, and usually enjoy the support of upper management

Numerous journal articles have reported on the psychological profiles of bullies: one series of studies posited that bullies have low levels of confidence and frequently attack those in the organization who have superior abilities (Vickers, 2006). However, Namie (2003) suggest that many bullies have the opposite profile - highly confident and empowered in their actions by their status within the organization. These opposing results are not mutually exclusive, as there is research indication that both perspectives are valid. Therefore, this wide range of bullying-motivating behavior creates an even more complex arrangement, as both low and excessive self-esteem can lead to treating coworkers as non-equals and therefore allowing for the development of deviant behavior. Suffice to say that the bully's psychological traits include aggression, intolerance and narcissism (Namie, 2007). Because bully behaviors are often implicitly condoned by management, and the bullies are adept at influencing colleagues, the successful bully is able to stigmatize targets, which results in the target being perceived as the source of the problem.

Hemmings' (2013) research concluded that there is a connection between the five variables of workplace environment, weak leadership, competition for advancement, envy, being different and workplace bullying. For the five variables, the study indicated that as the work environment improved the presence of bullying decreased, whereas when the phenomenon of weak leadership is present, competition for advancement, envy, and differences, increased, and the presence of bullying also increased.

Section 3: Understanding Terminology From The Bully World

Bullying. Bullying refers to the combination of verbal abuse and humiliating, threatening, or intimidating behaviors to the victim.

Downward bullying implies a form of workplace mobbing by a superior against a subordinate.

Empathy gap addresses the fundamental lack of understanding of the lived experience of the victim of bullying. This "empathy gap" can be demoralizing as it results in the victim not getting the support, intervention, or advocacy they need.

Hierarchal bullying reflects an infrequent form of bullying behavior which occurs in the hierarchy and is directed upward, from subordinate to superior.

Horizontal bullying suggest the types of bullying which occurs between individuals of equal power.

Instigator is one of the triad involved in bullying and is another term for **"perpetrator"**, which is less pejorative and reflects the intentionality of the bully behavior.

Mobbing. A group centered approach to bullying, and includes communication that is directed in a systematic way by more than one individual, toward another individual. These actions occur repeatedly, and on a sustained basis, over several months' duration.

Non-physical violence includes verbal abuse, intimidation, and threatening behavior which can adversely affect personal health and wellbeing.

Observer is one of the triad involved in bullying and is another term for **"witness"**, which is less pejorative and reflects unintended participance as a result of proximity.

Physical violence involves the use of force against another person or group that results in physical contact and harm, to include, beating, biting, blocking, elbowing, head butting, kicking, pinching, pushing, scratching, shoving, slapping, spitting, and stabbing.

Psychological terror includes hostile and unethical communications which are directed in a systematic way by one or a number of persons mainly towards one individual and can be deployed under the guise of formal complaint channels such as the ombudsman's office, an EEO office or filing an IG complaint.

Psychological violence includes misused power against another person or group which results in psychological harm or an incapacity to advance professionally. This includes, but is not limited to, non-physical violence bullying, emotional abuse, intimidation, suggestive behavior, threats of physical abuse, and verbal abuse.

Scapegoating represents the phenomenon of a situation where the focus of group aggression is directed towards an individual "blameless" entity; such as, a person or group who does not, in fact, intimidate or otherwise bother the main group.

Target is one of the triad involved in bullying and is another term for "**victim**", which is less pejorative and reflects the Helplessness of their plight.

Upward bullying is another name for mobbing up the ladder.

Workplace incivility. A low-intensity deviant behavior with ambiguous intent to harm the target in violation of workplace norms for mutual respect, although can be used to masquerade and obfuscate other more insidious intentions.

Workplace violence. An action or incident that physically or psychologically harms another person.

Section 4: Know Your Enemy, Know Yourself

The act of stopping the bully begins with the victim, the target, or the receiver of the abusive behavior each accepting that they have the power to impact the bully behavior towards making it stop. You have the power! You first have to understand what is happening, then what you can do about the bully behavior to make it stop. First you will have to change how you see yourself, then you will have to change how others see you and recognize how your bullying story inhibits you. Stopping the bully begins with understanding the bully behaviors and how the behaviors have confused you about your own power.

It is significant to note that workplace bullying is currently addressed within several research fields, including; business, education, health care, leadership, management, organizational theory, organizational behavior, organizational psychology, and social psychology. Understanding the complexity of bullying helps to prepare you to stop the behavior from harming you.

Bullies employ a variety of tactics, the most common of which is verbal abuse. Verbal abuse can occur in one-on-one situations or in front of the entire workgroup and include forms of speech from screaming to condescending statements.   This primary tactic is used in a large range of workplace settings. From my personal experience verbal bullying can quickly morph into cyberbullying, which includes using emails and other electronic communication vehicles to convey aggression. We all know the guy who sends out the flaming e-mails! And maybe we even know the girl who sends out the not-so-funny cartoon about which she has re-captioned to make light of her colleague Mary.

Story #4.   Barry And The Bully Senior Executive

Barry worked his whole adult life as a public servant, and he was a dedicated federal employee. Barry was committed to the agency's mission and he was always considered a solid performer. He was the kind of guy who you could count on to handle the routine and mundane work on a regular basis, but when needed he could jump in and handle a special project as a collateral duty without any fuss. That was just the way he was … a no-fuss kind of guy… a guy who you could always count on, a good guy!

Barry loved working on his own projects, and his customers were like family to him, as he often worked long hours during crunch time to ensure that their needs were met. Barry was a competent project manager, and he ensured that each of his projects remained in scope, on schedule and under budget. Life was simple, roles were clearly understood and Barry was a contributing and happy employee. Barry was an ideal worker, who thrived in his work environment. Not only did Barry manage his own workload, he always provided a helping hand, a positive attitude, and a supportive demeanor to his colleagues. Barry's cubicle also served as a haven for unhappy colleagues, who either personally or professionally needed a listening ear. Barry always took the time to listen to and comfort them, and to offer some constructive insight towards their dilemma.

Unfortunately Barry fell upon a professional mishap when he misinterpreted the significance of an e-mail communication from his senior executive. One of the projects that Barry was managing had significant political visibility, and was an integral part of the organizations long-term strategy to replace old dysfunctional buildings with state-of-the art platforms. Although Barry was not a player in terms of promoting himself or his accomplishments, he was generally attuned to the political nuances of the organization, and he understood the lines of demarcation relative to making any public statements about his projects. As a result of his unfamiliarity with managing any of the PR aspects of his projects, he did not recognize the significance of the senior executives' e-mail request to prepare a paragraph announcing the completion of one of his projects. Barry took the request on face value and assumed that the intent was satisfied when he notified the internal PR officer of the basic scope, schedule and budget of his project. Barry only provided the basics, no embellishment or detail. He did not elaborate on the technology, or the partnership, or the impending improved support to the mission that would be accomplished as a result of this new facility being commissioned.

There was no mal-intent here, as Barry was just-the-facts kind of guy. Barry was straight forward and to the point. Unfortunately, the information that Barry provided in response to the senior executive's request went to print from the PR officers' desk, and it completely missed the opportunity to showcase the project' or the accomplishments of Barry's division and chain of command. The senior executive went ballistic. The senior executives' initial outburst of verbal abuse towards Barry was public, was cruel, was personal, it was disproportionate to the crime, and it served to intentionally humiliate and demean an otherwise solid employee. Unfortunately the senior executive's bullying behavior did not stop with the berating reprimand, it took up a more personal and targeted assault. The bullying that Barry endured over the next several months was dreadful, and he began to wilt before his colleagues eyes. He was either excluded from relevant project meetings by the senior executive, or he was harangued during the meetings that he was in attendance at. The bully was like a dog with a bone and one which he could not let go of. Barry was the recipient of underserved verbal abuse and abusive commentary, and even when Barry was not present his bully continued to talk badly about him.

Barry became consumed by events around the initial incident (the abusive verbal assault), telling all who would listen that never before in his career had he been treated so badly. Barry's humiliation and shame was so public and so intense that even outside agencies were aware of Barry's flaming, such that Barry became a torch bearer for other organizations that sought to find fault or confirm their disdain for the offending senior executive. Human nature being as it is the folklore surrounding Barry's' public humiliation became more bold with each telling. Barry in turn commenced the inevitable death spiral after his public shaming. He changed from being a good performer to becoming the office malcontent, with reduced organizational dedication and output. Barry purposely and deliberately withdrew his work effort, and his other projects began to suffer. His work attendance, which had always been stellar, also began to deteriorate. Mondays and Fridays became recurring "sick-days" for Barry, and when he did work he purposely decreased the work quality. Barry contemplated filing a hostile work environment complaint, but after he examined the situation rationally he accepted that there would be no resolution for him if he did. The predominant thought that prevented Barry from filing a complaint about the senior executive's bully behavior was that this was not the first occurrence of bullying behavior that the senior executive had conducted. It came to light that there were numerous other victims scattered around the organization that had fallen within reach of the bully. Barry knew that nothing had been done in the past to stop this bullying behavior, so why would his complaint make any difference now. Barry recognized and thus accepted the complacent and permissive organizational structures, which permitted the continuation of the bullying behaviors. As Barry counted the body's strewn around the campus, he realized that the organization tacitly condoned the bully's deviant behavior, for how could the bully have endured so long and so well otherwise? Armed with the belief that no one would give a rat's ass about his plight, he just sucked it up and began to look for another job.

A happy ending for the organization would have been if Barry had elected to changed jobs quickly, unfortunately as a career federal employee that is not so easily accomplished. Although Barry actively searched for other assignments, the process moved slowly, and Barry was now an item of curiosity. Unfortunately, experience shows that such curiosity and speculation falls more harshly on the victim than on the bully aggressor, and Barry languished in the organization while his once supportive demeanor was gradually replaced with a hostile and belligerent one. Eventually however, and with great good luck Barry secured a lateral moved to another division, and understandably he spewed venom when asked about his old senior executive. The new division provided Barry ample opportunity and top cover to settle old scores, as he was able to influence perceptions, conversations and resources that related to the domain of his old job. What Barry could not do overtly when he worked for the bully in terms of rebalancing power and securing revenge, he managed to conclude stealthily when he was out of the line of fire and in his new job.

Almost four years later the bully senior executive resigned under a cloud of scrutiny, and loss of power and influence, while Barry has survived and returned to a happier version of his former high performing self; although neither Barry nor the organization has been made completely whole.

Verbal attacks in front of peers and subordinates is another popular tactic of the bully, because this approach usually results in purposeful social ostracism. Barry in the story above endured chronic bullying; however Barry never said STOP! Not that saying STOP is easy, but as with everything else in life if we don't ask then we don't get. So Barry did not take the first step in stopping the bully from bullying him, and he did not take back his power.

Bullies seek to degrade their targets by turning colleagues against them and destroying the targets 'workplace relationship. As if the lone bully was not insidious enough, the *group* process of bullying a fellow worker has taken on a life of its own and has been termed mobbing.   Mobbing occurs when leadership fails. Leadership fails when either the leader who is leading the pack, condones the mobbing behavior, or fails to stop the behavior, or fails to recognize there is a problem. Charismatic leaders have been known to influence subordinates toward inappropriate acts, including mobbing. I have witnessed a senio bully leader consistently speak disparagingly about another federal organization, with such venom and frequency that the internal sycophants frequently repeated the commentary as if it was their own opinion and experience. As a result we were forced to endure a very long period of non-engagement with fellow federal employees from the other organization, as we had become a pariah organization as a result of the bully behavior of one particular leader.

Story #5.   Steve, The Bombastic and Bullying Screamer

Steve was a bombastic and bullying screamer. When things didn't go his way he lost control of his emotions and screamed. On a good day Steve was a kind, considerate, intelligent and sometimes thoughtful executive, at least that's how he would and could behave towards his immediate workgroup. However, when things did not go the way Steve wanted, he had acquired a very bad habit of screaming at whoever delivered him the bad news. Steve had the ability to run hot and cold with people in his work group. One day you were in the inner circle and high on his list of go-to people. However, if you disagreed with him (i.e. did not see things his way) you were immediately eliminated from the inner-circle, and reduced to a sad existence living outside the bosses' clique. Everyone knew who was who, and who was in, and who was where within the

Steve is still a bombastic and bullying screamer, however he is without influence these days, as no one from the new guard will bring him bad news. He has recently been relieved of his more prestigious projects, and he is now professionally isolated and without influence. Unfortunately, there is not yet a happy ending here, as Steve remains deeply unaware that his bombastic and bullying behavior, and horrendous emotional outbursts, are the cause of his declining professional stance and influence. Did Steve fail

Steve himself by not taking to heart the coaching and training he was provided by the organization, or did his loyal companions and the organization fail him for not hammering his lack of awareness about the unacceptability of his bullying behavior. Either way Steve's behavior has become a career ender, as somewhere along the way the organization heard enough complaints about Steve and his behavior that they finally said stop!

Bully leaders often exhibit narcissistic personalities, and these traits impact the culture of the organizations. The philosophies of the leader becomes the dominant ideology of the organization, and alternative perspectives and opposing views are marginalized. Frequently the bully leader uses his coercive power to influence his team members toward a certain outcome, such as abusive group behavior. Steve's narcissistic personality directly impacted the culture and perspective of his organization.

you retell me this story, what are you experiencing at this moment..."I am feeling shame! I am ashamed still that this happened to me. Me! I am somebody in this organization, and this jerk treated me like a piece of shit.... and now all I want to do is punch him in the face right now for taking away my sense of who I am!"

Mary was traumatized by her bully Jim, but what was the impact upon her organization? Intuitively and factually we recognize that organizations experiencing occurrences of workplace bullying, incivility and deviant behavior endure increased employee turnover, employee absenteeism, increased health insurance claims, reduced productivity, reduced supportive behavior among peers, and damage to both organizational and individual reputations. Research also indicates that employees enduring a deviant or bullying work environment are less satisfied, less cooperative, and less courteous than their counterparts in organizations imbued with a positive and civil culture. From an organizational perspective it goes without saying that workplace bullying, rudeness and incivility is bad for business, and adversely reflects upon the company's bottom line.

Story #7.   Mary Does Not Trust Jim

Mary, where did you go from this point onwards in your relationship with Jim? Jim is a jerk! In my mind that will never change... I don't care how many coaches you hire for him. I don't believe you can really empower people to do their job unless you trust them to make good choices...and Jim made it clear that he did not respect or trust me, so where was I to go as a follower? What was I to do? Mary, do you trust Jim? Hell No! No Way!! No I do not trust Jim, and as a follower you need to trust your leader, don't you? We have come to this place you see, this arrangement, where I won't bring Jim any information on my project, as I don't trust him to be supportive of my perspective, or my need for resources, and besides I just don't want to get yelled at again! This is not middle school and I refuse to be treated like a child. I am good at what I do and won't be disrespected again by that jerk Jim. Mary, do you own any aspect of rebuilding the relationship with Jim. No, nope. ... .absolutely not... I do not! Jim is a dickhead and I want nothing to do with him.   Mary, does Jim have the resources you need to make your project successful? Well yes……………., but when I see him I just want to punch him in the face…so I won't ask him for anything. Mary, how long can you sustain this way of thinking and how is it affecting your enjoyment here at work? God, I am screwed am I not.   But what else can I do!?

Mary does not trust Jim any more. Bullying and bully behavior undermines organizational trust. The question here is what does Mary do about telling Jim to stop his abusive behavior? Mary carries ill will towards Jim and now the work relationship is destroyed. Mary avoids the bully, but Mary does not appear ready to manage the relationship and tell the bully to STOP.

Section 5: What is workplace bullying and what do I need to know?

Both experiencing and observing bullying behaviors frequently accelerates our learning and understanding about what the phenomenon of bullying is.

Story #8.   Jane And The New Hire, Dick.

Jane arrived at her workplace every day full of dread of whatever new cruelties her colleague would bring her, for poor Jane worked with a bully. Jane began each morning arising from her bed exhausted after a fruitless night of tossing and turning, and gnashing and grinding her teeth. Her husband was at his wits end because he did not understand why she let this asshole disrupt her happiness and bring misery into their home. Each morning Jane arose from her bed feeling guilty for another night of disharmony in her home, and another day of not being the joyful and loving wife and friend she used to be. As Jane prepared for work she was keenly aware that she looked bedraggled and felt exhausted, however she did not have the emotional energy to present a better face or appearance to the outside world. Her health was impacted. Her hair was thinning, her skin was patchy, she had lost weight in her face, her nails were chipped and chewed to the quick, and her clothes were hanging off her like some sad mannequin from a second-hand store. She simply felt beaten down and that is exactly how she looked.

Although Jane is a gentle soul she was a much sought after member of the team because her particular skills required deep contemplation and reflection. Her story had been very different prior to last summer, for Jane use to truly enjoy her job and the people she worked with. The old Jane was fun-loving and generous both at home and at work, and often invested additional effort in ensuring that those around her were well cared for. However, last March after an extended period of professional stability, Jane's boss hired another analyst because of the growing demand for analysis. In addition to the additional workload, the boss also wanted to introduce a new computer system, so there was a steep learning curve for the entire department and productivity was expected to be impacted, thus the new hire was even more appreciated.

Jane welcomed the new guy – his name was Dick. They were quiet similar in terms of professional experience, education and age – there seemed many reasons to believe that Dick should have been a great addition to the team. However, shortly after his arrival Jane found herself purposely and intentionally avoiding Dick, for what appeared to be the most mundane of reasons. Dick had a certain way about him that just rubbed everyone the wrong way. However, Dick was a high achiever, and the boss loved him. Dick appeared to very subtly enjoy tormenting his colleagues when they didn't or couldn't immediately learn how to manage the new computer technology. Dick had other nasty habits too, and made Jane the target of his daily tirade. Dick enjoyed making snide comments about Jane loudly, such that she could hear him talking about her to others. Dick would challenge Jane openly about her work product or her professional perspective, and never in a particularly courteous or professional way. Dick would cut Jane out of the conversation during team meetings, and undermine her credibility in front of her boss and other colleagues. Dick would use patronizing language towards Jane, and his derisiveness was direct and specific, such as …"well now Jane, while that's a lovely idea we have serious work to do here and have to put our big-boy thinking hats on to solve this problem…" Dick would also tell their respective customers that he had the answers they needed and to avoid bringing issues to Jane, as she was "swamped". The list of crap that Jane endured from Dick was endless, and never in her professional career had she experienced such objectionable behavior directed at her.

The boss, who was under pressure to rapidly implement the new computer technology, appeared to tacitly condone Dick's behavior towards the group in general, and towards Jane specifically. The boss acted as if Dick's behavior was benign and merely a harmless cajoling of the workgroup in order to get them to accelerate their learning and implementation of the new technology. As for Jane, well the boss always thought she was a bit too thin-skinned, and that Dick's harmless cajoling of her would toughen her up! Jane however saw things very differently, and she purposely became distant and less productive as she stepped back from fully engaging with the team. Jane wasted what little energy she had left living in a constant state of worry and anxiety. The boss became aware of her reduced organizational dedication, and now he was pissed off at her. He started to see her as a slacker, and perhaps Dick had been right in *his observations about Jane. Maybe she was in over her head, and it took a sharp guy like Dick to illuminate just how under skilled Jane was.   Her colleagues wondered about her reduced output, although they recognized that she was avoiding Dick-The-Bully, they were frustrated by her lack of team engagement, and wished she would just suck it up and get on with it!   Jane however, could not just suck it up! She began taking more sick-days and was chastised by her boss for this. After a period of time Jane went to HR to seek assistance, however when they looked at her personal file (full of recent counseling's by her boss for absence, tardiness and poor output) all they saw was a chronic malinger and weak employee, who had started the inevitable downward slide towards termination.*

In hindsight, Jane should have confronted her bully abuser immediately, and also go on notice with her boss and HR about the bullying behavior she was enduring. However, as we all know that is very seldom the sequence of events in a typical workplace bullying saga, and the victim of bullying will be re-victimized by the organization performance expectations and processes.

Q# 1. What is a workplace bully?

Jane's story above is a common experience of workplace bullying. For the sake of simplicity, a workplace bully is basically anyone who makes your work life a living hell by contributing to or creating, a hostile, abusive or intolerable work environment. This is usually accomplished through intimidation, humiliation, criticism and ridicule, or demeaning behavior.

Q# 2. What should I know about bullies?

Learn what a bully is and what a bully does. Just like their horrid little brothers and sisters on the school playground, workplace bullies use the same means of intimidation and influence to bring you down to their level. Learn how to recognize their behavior, as this is the first step in defending yourself and staying safe in your workplace. Without distinction it is difficult to know what something is, and then it will be too late to avoid the consequences. Most people who encounter a bully did not know what the phenomenon was, or how insidious bully behavior is, until it happens to them personally. Jane endured a quick tutorial above about bullying when she experienced Jack's abusive behavior.

Q# 3. What are common bullying behaviors?

Common bully behaviors include condescending remarks and repeated sarcasm, demeaning back-slapping, denial or removal of normal privileges, denying credit and acknowledgement for work done, excessive scrutiny and micromanaging, harsh expressions and looks, fake punching, elbowing, false or exaggerated allegations, getting in your face, hand gestures, hostile tones, inappropriate touching, invading personal space, malicious gossip, name-calling, pushing, recurring cold shoulder, relentless criticism, shouting, social ostracism, swearing obscenities, threats and threatening behaviors, unreasonable demands (by complexity or timeliness), unwarranted reprimands, and vicious or insipid put-downs.

Q# 4. What Are Some Other Forms Of Workplace Bullying?

Some of the more passive-aggressive, subtle and lesser known bullying behaviors include, purposeful exclusion from team meetings or group activities, consistently stealing your limelight or credit for your work, overloading you with busy work, purposely withholding information from your team, sabotaging your work effort, spreading false rumors and gossiping, taking away all of your meaningful work (then stating that you are under performing), and withholding pertinent information from higher authorities.

Q# 5. How would I know if I am being bullied?

Pay attention. There will be signs outside of your workplace that suggest you are the target of workplace bullying. You are suffering from workplace bullying if you hurt at home in the following way. You experience trouble sleeping. You frequently struggle with nausea and vomiting, especially when you think about work. Your family are frustrated because of your non-stop obsessing about your work problems. You takeoff sick days when you are not actually sick. When you are away from the office for a few days you are already worrying about having to go back to work. Your doctor observes health challenges and changes, such as problems with blood pressure, heart rate, hair and skin condition, digestion and metabolism. You feel guilty and ashamed for invoking a disharmonious work environment.

Q# 6. Are there different types of bullies in the workplace?

Basically there are three frequent types of bullies in your workplace. Firstly, there are bully customers who can create havoc on a transactional level, only so long as you must engage with them. Secondly there are bully coworkers who can disrupt your daily work-life and make your life miserable. Thirdly, there is the bully bosses, who can screw up your career. There is a fourth character in the bully workplace drama that is seldom spoken about, and that is the subordinate. The subordinate who is powerful by association or tenure, he is usually well connected and he knows how to obfuscate malicious intention behind structural programs, such as EEO, IG or other complaint channels. The subordinate exercises hierarchal bullying and his reach and influence is both insidious and treacherous, and he usually seeks out new appointees who he feels are in positions that he was denied, and his intentions are to unseat and undermine the new appointee. However, don't let there be any doubt that the most widespread damage occurs as a result of the bully boss, who unlike with bully coworkers, can cause you harm when you stand up for yourself. Bully bosses by virtue of their position in the organization, hold more substantial power over you than other bullies.

Q# 7. If I am being bullied is it my fault?

Absolutely not! You must understand that a bullying act against you is never your fault. Every bully is weak and acts from a place
of cowardness. Whenever you experience bullying, or witness bullying, remember, the bully is a weak and cowardly specimen, even if they appear stronger and with lots of organizational power. Bullies inherently are attempting to assuage their own insecurities and feelings of weakness through the act of bullying.   Always remember that bullies are merely cowards in false positions of power.

Q# 8. Should I just accept the bullying behavior because it is my fault?

Never accept the belief that someone can hurt you because of something you have (not) done. Some bullies at work will criticize you in a bad way and make it sound like they are doing you a favor. Bullying is never right even if you did something wrong. Trying to convince you that you "deserve" this behavior is also a form of abuse.

Q# 9. Does my inherent niceness contribute to bullying?

Don't be too nice. Plain and simply don't be a doormat – if you are a doormat people will walk all over you and wipe their feet on you. Peer or horizontal bullying is the most difficult to overcome, because we all make an extra effort to be nice to our peer colleagues. If you are being bullied by a group of colleagues, you must resist the urge to appease the group that has abused you. You must not role over or try to do them favors with the expectation that they will cease their bullying behavior. They will not and you are just feeding their belief that they are strong. Experience shows that bullied targets are frequently too nice for their own good, which makes them more prone to being bullied more frequently than others. I am not suggesting that you now show up as a thug or a bitch at work, but just don't be an overly nice doormat.

Q# 10. So, do all bullies mean to bully?

I do not assume to suggest that all bullies purposely mean to be mean. I have observed and researched that some management styles are closer to bully behavior than the leader may be aware. Lack of self-awareness is an integral part of bully behavior and personality.   I recommend you talk to the person and request to give them feedback on how their behavior is affecting you. As an executive coach I suggest that you never offer feedback without first requesting permission. It goes something like this…. "..Jim, yesterday when you spoke to me I was quiet upset about your delivery. May I offer you some specific feedback about how your behavior affected me and how I would prefer you to treat me and to behave in my presence? I don't believe you intended to bully me, however that is how I experienced our exchange …" If this scares you, then practice the conversation on a trusted friend or use a visualization technique (such as speaking to a photograph of the bully) to give you confidence.

Q# 11. Does a bully enjoy tormenting others?

Yes, a purposeful bully gains enjoyment from tormenting others. Distinguish between the purposeful and the accidental bully by recognizing this trait - does the instigator seem to make special effort in disturbing your happiness, tripping you up professionally, or bringing you down emotionally? Do they seem to enjoy it? If your gut answer is yes, this jerk is a purposeful bully.

Q# 12. What goes on in a bully's head?

While none of us know what really goes on inside another person's head, from research we do know that bullies often have deep-seated psychological issues related to identity and control. Understand that the bullying behavior you endure has less to do with how you show up in the workplace and more to do with the bully's own demons and insecurities. Not that his insecurities should ever be an excuse for his abhorrent behavior.

Q# 13. Is the quality of my work performance a reason to be bullied?

Do a good job, certainly do the best job you can, because your best effort will minimize the target of opportunities a bully has against you.   Much of your status as an employee in the organization is based on the quality of your work, so don't expose your flank by performing shoddily. Also be attentive with time and attendance.   Be seen to work the required number of hours, clocking in and out as required. When you are experiencing excessive scrutiny a protective technique is to e-mail your boss or another senior person immediately upon arrival in the morning to memorialize your presence in the workspace. This will serve as an audit trail in the event that your time and attendance patterns ever becomes an issue. Likewise either send the boss or even yourself an e-mail at the end of each workday with some innocuous note such, as your to-do list for the next day. Be sure to arrive at meetings on time, and be prepared and mentally present, and deliver your work to the agreed schedule.   When you are given task by the bully be sure to memorialize and follow up with an e-mail asking for confirmation of your understanding of the scope and schedule of the task. This way you are building in another layer of protection. Furthermore, it will decrease the amount of opportunities the bully has to find fault against you.

Q# 14. Is all poor, or offensive, or uncomfortable behavior considered bullying?

No, not all deviant behavior is considered to be bullying. On the spectrum of deviant workplace behavior incivility and uncivil behavior occupies the lowest end. Incivility is distinctive from bullying by its ambiguous intent to harm, albeit results in hurtful or damaging behavior. Bullying is distinctive by its purposeful intent to harm. Along the same spectrum of deviant workplace behavior, the acts of violence and murder are on the opposite end to incivility and bullying. Learn to recognize and place deviant behaviors along the entire spectrum, and review each action as a discrete activity. Not every conflicted engagement in the workplace is bullying. Your supervisor may need to make sure you are doing your job when they alert you to a deficiency in your work, however that aspect of the supervisor/subordinate relationship is necessary for the proper functioning of the organization and therefore it is not considered downward bullying.

Q# 15. What do I do when I endure the experience of verbal bullying?

When there is verbal bullying, ignore it! Do not engage! Do not say anything in return because this indicates that you are vulnerable and affected by the words that are thrown at you. This is how the bully first knows he is getting to you. One of my many great mentors gave me sage advice when I young and early in my career. **"… Don't wrestle with pigs, for three reasons. First reason is that the pig likes it, the second reason is that you will get dirty, and the third reason is that after a while people on the outside looking in won't be able to tell who is who…"** If you catch yourself being sucked in to the bullies' negative vortex remind yourself of the pig wrestling analogy and pull yourself back!

Story #9.   Fred and Ginger

The work is demanding and the team is spirited, the boss enjoys the banter with the team as he supposes that he understands the dynamic of the group and recognizes that they are just letting off steam. They are usually self-policing and pull each other aside if the banter is getting too intense towards any one person on the team. Fred believes he has a handle on things where the team is concerned. Fred's team was tasked to develop a new process in conjunction with another workgroup, so he invited the entire group and their leader Ginger over for a day-long workshop. The workshop was going well until Ginger stood up to speak. Fred witnessed his people passing notes back and forth during Ginger's presentation, and saying unkind things about her appearance…wow he thought, we are not in high school anymore so what is the problem? Fred pulled his guys aside and directed them to knock it off! Upon further reflection Fred wondered if his own behavior as a leader and his willingness to tolerate and even enter into the playful banter with his team gave them license to act so badly towards another team.

Q# 16. Should I engage with those who verbally upset me?

When someone hurls verbal abuse at you, stay calm! Bullies have a keen ability of knowing if they have gotten under your skin - so fake it if you have to. Whatever happens, do not engage - do not fight back! Take a deep breath! Sstate in a calm slow and clear voice that "you may not speak to me in that manner, and I refuse to listen to you until you have regained your composure…" Beware of the phenomenon Daniel Goleman (1996) described as "…*Amygdala hijacking*…" from his book on Emotional Intelligence. Goleman used the term to describe emotional responses from people which are intense, immediate, and overwhelming, and out of measure with the actual stimulus because it has triggered a much more significant emotional threat. Responding aggressively is what the bully wants you to do, it is what he needs to feed his rage and therefore he will try to draw you into the conflict. Did you know that when a dog has bitten into your arm you must lift him up by the tail to get him to release his grip? You see, he has no traction when he is suspended by his tail. Likewise do allow your bully to gain traction by responding directly to his verbal assault.

Q# 17. How do bullies select their targets?

Unlike playground bullies, who picked on targets they saw as alone or weak, workplace bullies typically pick upon more competent employees, which they consider to be a threat to their career. If your professional presence or demeanor (even unintentionally) makes someone else look bad, the natural bully will feel the need to take you down. This explains the underreported phenomenon of hierarchal bullying, which is subordinate initiated or upward bullying of new appointees. The bully fears uppity colleagues who have moved ahead of them professionally, or new appointees that were assigned to higher positions that the bully thought should have naturally been his. As a coach I would advise you to be wary of accepting a position in a new organization where the "acting" incumbent was not selected for the position and now must report to you. Human nature, as well as jealousy, envy and pride, when combined with inherent personality weaknesses of a bully represent a travesty waiting to happen.

Q# 18. As a target of bullying am I alone?

Typically not - although not always in the same space or time. If you are being bullied, there is a good chance that others are or have also been abused by this bully. Do your homework and locate the other victims, past and present, and team up with them and help each other in the face of the common enemy.

Q# 19. Is it possible to recover from bullying?

Yes – recovering from the trauma of being bullied is a process, so make getting better your priority. I recommend one of two avenues, however you have other choices available to you such as your pastor or spiritual leader. Firstly, I recommend a workplace coach, otherwise known as an executive or leadership coach. Coaching will help you become a more skillful observer of yourself. Secondly I would alternatively recommend a mental health professional if the trauma of the bullying experience reopened previously endured stressful episodes in your life. I don't presume to speak knowledgeably about PTSD, however I am familiar with its significance in workplace bully situations. Your effectiveness as an employee and worker is diminished, and you won't be happy or joyful in yourself if you don't take the time to confront and recover from your bullying experience. Take some time off and ignore work for a while.

Q# 20. Is gossip a form of bullying?

Yes, malicious gossip is a form of bullying. Beware of malicious gossip and unkind remarks that are dressed up as jokes or "harmless" banter. If it hurts your feelings, it hurts your feelings – not because you are thin-skinned, but because it just hurts your feelings.

Q# 21. How does the instigator reconcile his bullying behavior?

A bully or instigator has proven methods to rationalize his deviant behavior in the workplace. The phenomenon of rationalizing antisocial behavior has a long history, more recently during WWII with the systematic annihilation of Jews, PolPots' atrocities during the Cambodian genocide, Rwanda's genocide, and the Bosnia and Herzegovina ethnic troubles. Many attempts were made by the perpetrators to recast these atrocities to a more acceptable activity.

Research has established that the perpetrators of antisocial or uncivil behaviors typically use up to five different approaches to reduce public outrage, to include covering up the activity against the target; devaluation of the humanity of the target; reinterpretation of the event to a more acceptable activity; hiding behind official processes or procedures; and intimidation and bribery where targets and observers of the incident are threatened or otherwise incentivized to be silent. The same five methods are employed by bullies to reduce outrage and reconcile their deviant behavior. A bully typically refrains from bullying a target while in the presence of his own peers or superiors, while returning to his abusive ways after their departure. A bully boss who practices the art of downward bullying can arbitrarily take away a targets duties and reduce their scope of responsibilities with the intent and effect of diminishing their professional stance in the organization. A bully boss can reassign the target to an unfavorable or undesired assignment; and then make a public announcement about how the new assignment is intended to be a plum or stretch assignment for the good of the individual and the organization (this is BS that you can usually smell a mile away).   A bully boss claims that the targets' work is not up to expected performance standards and withholds a bonus or a promotion through the strictures of the annual personnel evaluation system. Targets are often silenced by the power strictures the bully boss holds over their professional development, as he can withhold or grant developmental assignments depending upon how they play along with his game.

Q# 22. Can complaints of bullying be unfounded?

Yes, some bullying complaints are indeed unfounded. Some workers who claim they've been bullied have actually been treated reasonably in the context of their own behavior, performance, and organizational norms.   Some of them are bullies themselves and typically lack self-awareness and possess an overestimation of their own skills and abilities.   They see tiny flaws in others' behavior but not the larger flaws in their own, and frequently cry foul or file a bullying complaint when their own performance or professional expectations are not satisfied.

Q# 23. Do all bullies know how they are impacting others?

Some people who regularly use bullying behaviors have no idea what effect they're having on others, and these are referred to as unintended bullies and usually lack deep self-awareness. If they are fortunate someone finally tells them, so when they really understand they are embarrassed, and may even thank whoever told them. If you've been bullied by such a person, the solution is simple and direct, though repeated messages may be necessary to help change poor workplace habits. A colleague of mine was accused of being aggressive towards a contract employee. He entered their cubicle space uninvited and proceeded to hotly discuss a problem as he remained standing inside the cubicle opening and they were sitting down. He was astonished by their response when they lodged a bullying complaint against him. I sat him down and drew him a three-dimensional picture of his perceived behavior inside the cubicle, (a 6X6 sized cubicle), and only then did he understand the dynamics within the small space that had occurred and caused the individual to feel abused. He was deeply apologetic.

Q# 24. Is the bully capable of changing?

Yes, a bully can be helped to change –if they are open to feedback and training in self-awareness. Unfortunately, many instigators are often unable to change, because they lack deep self-awareness, or because of their narcissistic tendencies they don't believe there is a problem therefore they do not want to change (as he is happy with the fabulous version of himself that he had created). In some cases, requiring the bully to change (or else) can make things a lot worse for the organization, as the clever ones go underground and become more covert in their bullying behavior. Be wary of reformed bullies!

Q# 25. How do bullies appear to so easily unnerve their targets?

Bullies are clever bastards! That is why they are able to be effective bullies, as the endeavor of being a bully is their own personal workplace game. Bullies are often skilled in finding weaknesses in their targets, simply because they are practiced bullies, and have been behaving in this manner for most of their life. Even a fool can learn to recognize patterns after a while. Bullies know how to needle targets until they find a weak layer and crack it wide open. Targets then typically either implode and succumb to the bullying, or blow up in anger. Either way the bully counts the encounter as a success. If the bully is sufficiently subtle, observers may think the target is the only one causing a problem (consider my pig wrestling analogy above).

Q# 26. Do bullies interpret their actions as unfair?

Nope - it is not in their makeup to view their own actions as unfair, although they are prone to viewing another's milder actions to be unfair when it impacts them. With the evidence of hostile actions being undeniable, bullies and their allies frequently attempt to explicate themselves from any wrongdoing, by rationalizing their own actions and implying that the victim was somehow responsible for the negative engagement. To withstand these schemes and rationalizations (bullies are clever bastards after all), you have to remain firm on the unfairness aspect of their actions. Calling a bully a bully can have a temporary chilling effect on him, but you also need to be firm in laying out the specific deviant and unacceptable behaviors.   Sometimes it is best to make specific pronouncements, such as "…Jim, your bullying behavior includes forcing your unrealistic expectations upon the workgroup…", or "…screaming like a maniac at a low level employee in the most unprofessional manner is unacceptable…", or "…making snide and sarcastic comments about the employee is unacceptable…"

Q# 27. Does the bully always attempt to blame someone else?

When confronted about his deviant workplace behavior, the purposeful bully will usually attempt to blame the reason for his actions on someone else, and usually it is the target who he will blame.   "…If Larry was not such a screw-up, with regards to the PR aspect of his project, I would not need to ride his the way I do…", or "…if you hadn't asked so many questions during the scoping phase of the project I would have been confident in your abilities and not transferred your project to Mike…".

Q# 28. Is there a surprising truth about what bullies really want?

All employees in the workplace aspire for the same three things; autonomy, mastery and purpose. The bully is no different, except that he just wants to achieve these three statuses in his own personal and often deviant way. Furthermore, he will strive to deny you your own realization of these aspirations out of jealousy, envy and other personal demons and insecurities. If the bully aspires for autonomy in his function yet does not have it he will never permit you to have it. If the bully aspires for mastery of an area that you are a master in, he will surely deny your abilities and undermine your credibility in that specific area. Once you figure out what your own personal bully wants or needs, you can choose to take possession of the board game if you want to. You now have the tools to shift the bully from wanting what you have to owning it himself, by permitting him to take some element ownership of your accomplishments for example. For example when being recognized by superiors for your specific technical accomplishments you can affirm the bullies own mastery by saying something like "… Well, if it hadn't been for my bosses' leadership and insight I would never have had the opportunity to help our team achieve this forward progress…" Is this the stance of a sycophant or a pragmatist, ultimately this is your decision alone to make as you navigate for survival in the domain of a bully.

Q# 29. What are some of the symptoms a target of bullying might

experience?

Some of the symptoms a target of bullying might experience include, clinical depression, debilitating anxiety, hypertension, migraine headaches, panic attacks, relapse of previously controlled addictions, severe mood swings, sleeplessness, ulcers, even post-traumatic stress disorder.

Story #10.   Tina And The Crazy Lunatic

In 1982 I worked in an engineering office in Frankfurt, Germany. My boss was a crazy lunatic who enjoyed his ability to exercise downward bullying. No joke! He was a chain smoker, yet he was a lung cancer survivor with only one lung. He was crazy! I was 21 years old and to me he appeared to be 100 years old at the time. He was a tall ferocious looking man and always wore a dark grey suit, white shirt and black tie. Needless to say I was terrified of him. Among about fifty Germans, there were three other non-Germans working alongside me; including two other Irish guys and an English guy. The Crazy Lunatic use to terrorize every engineer in the office, however he appeared to take particular delight in skewering us four non-Germans. Naturally, the four of us developed a very close camaraderie in the face of his incessant and abusive behavior, as we felt we were very fortunate to have such well-paying jobs right out of college. Thus we were determined to tough it out. I recall one particular day the Crazy Lunatic had summoned the four of us into the conference room to berate us over some perceived shortcoming. I was 21 and becoming fearless in the face of this incessant and abusive bully behavior, so I politely and diplomatically took umbrage at what the Crazy Lunatic was accusing us off. I declared that we most certainly had not behaved in the manner he described. At this point the Crazy Lunatic directed his viciousness towards me and stated that "… your problem young lady is that you need a boyfriend…" to which I retorted that I had one, thank you very much! His response was priceless and unforgettable, as he then suggested that "…obviously then you need a more adequate one…" implying that I needed to be F$#@!D! I was astounded, yet too naïve and stupid to think that this was something I should complain to HR about. I was already considered a second-class citizen, as I was not a member of the predominant national workgroup, thus I believed I had to endure this bullying behavior. I moved on from this crazy workplace, but I have never

Q# 30. What will happen if I don't deal with my bully?

When you are dealing with and experiencing the phenomenon of workplace bullying, I am here to tell you that the consequences of the experience you are enduring will remain with you for years to come. So, unless you take action today to put a stop to the bully in your workplace from disrupting your life and preventing you from experiencing your highest and best self, your suffering will continue to expand. Simply put - do something today to stop the madness, for every day that passes empowers the bully more and makes him more difficult to deal with later.

Section 6: What Should I do To Engage the Bully?

Q# 31. If I confront the bully what argument should I make?

If and when you are ready to confront your bully, be sure to make a bottom-line argument. Do not, under any circumstances, speak to the hurt, pain, suffering or psychological damage you have endured. This approach would diminish your powerfulness and make you look weak, and even suggests that perhaps your poor treatment by the bully was justified. Present the issue in economic impact terms and describe how the specific behavior, such as the deliberate refusal to communicate and share information inhibits the project being completed, or tasks being finished on time. The reason you are requesting him to cease and desist this behavior must not appear to be about your needs, rather it must be about the needs of the organization.

Q# 32. What should I do after I confront the bully?

Congratulations on your courage, however after you confront your bully realistically you should brace yourself for retaliation. Retaliation is in the bullies' nature and you have undermined their sense of powerlessness so they must now lash out at you. Most likely he will retaliate in covert and subtle ways, thereby making it difficult for you to draw a clear line between your actions and his retaliatory response. Likewise, you will not be able to adequately document his retaliation or relay his abusive response to HR, as you will be grasping at threads. Go on notice with your organization by letting them know your fears and concerns. You are doing your part for the organization by confronting the bully so as to prevent escalation. Remind the organization that escalation as a result of retaliation will result in both diminished performance and a possible future lawsuit. Go on record by asking the company specifically their policy on retaliation. This way they now have a duty of care to ensure compliance with their own policy.

Q# 33. Should I talk directly to the manager about his bullying behavior?

Yes, you owe it to yourself (and perhaps the manager too) to raise awareness about his bullying. However, when you speak to the manager about the bullying behavior, refrain from talking about your feelings. In many instances bullied targets are not heard when they complain because they focus the discussion on themselves and how they have been impacted, rather than the impact upon the organization.

Q# 34. Should I attempt to offer solutions in the face of enduring or observing bullying behavior?

Be the leader you are destined to be,+

 and lead from where you stand in the organization. So yes, you should offer solutions in the face of enduring or observing bullying behavior. Be explicit when you describe what you want from management in exchange for your observations and solutions. Explain that you are seeking training for your team in response to their recent deviant behaviors.   Explain that as a target of bullying you are seeking an interdepartmental transfer or that you want to secure coaching for the bully.

Q# 35. Should I ever give the bully the benefit of the doubt?

It is in our nature to give most people the benefit of the doubt at least once. If the bully is an accidental bully then yes, give him the benefit of the doubt. It might be possible that he doesn't know that he is upsetting you. Begin by letting him know that you find his behavior abusive and then ask him politely to desist. Often, this makes the accidental bully take stock of the way he has been behaving. Be specific and be direct. If you don't ask you don't get! If you know the bully to be an intentional bully do not, under any circumstance, give him the benefit of the doubt. Cut him off immediately and remove yourself from the conversation.

Q# 36. Should I engage the bully?

This must be your call as to whether you are emotionally ready to engage your bully. If you are ready then ask once, then ask a second time, to stop the abusive behavior if she does not respond to your first request. Remind the bully that you have already asked them once to desist and now you are asking them again, followed by the assertion that if the abusive behavior continues, you will lodge a complaint with someone above her in the organization.

Q# 37. Should I complain to my superior or to senior management?

Yes, both. I agree that you should complain to both your superior and to your senior management. Make your complaint a formal complaint, not just a comment in passing. Many targets make the fundamental mistake of "discussing" their plight with someone higher up in the chain and then assume that they have made a formal complaint. Be specific. State that you are making a specific complaint. Maintain both your professionalism and your calm demeanor when you present your complaint.

Q# 38. If I am being bullied what are the first steps I should take to stop the abuse?

The first step in stopping the bully abuse you are enduring is in recognizing and admitting you are being bullied. You should explore the antecedence and consequences of workplace bullying and recognize the players, especially the perpetrator, who can be a manager, peers, customers, colleagues or even subordinates. Ask yourself a series of questions as follows: (1) would I accept this abusive behavior from a stranger. (2) Would I accept this abusive behavior from a family member?" If the answer is no, then you probably are being bullied.

Q# 39. How to I deal with bullying if it's happening to me?

Unfortunately, bullies are adept at knowing and exploiting your weak points. Confuse the bully by behaving in an assertive, strong manner, even if you don't feel that way inside. And no matter how hard they push, don't show them that you are upset. It's no fun bullying someone who doesn't react, and so the bad behavior often stops or is redirected elsewhere.

Q# 40. Should I introduce humor in the face of bullying?

Yes, humor is a sign of strength and confidence, so find funny things to say in the face of bullying. Humor is a good way to diffuse tensions and diminish an act of bullying and puts you in control of the stage.

Q# 41. Should I take my bullying business home with me?

Keep the bully blues out of your house and home. Do not take your anger and frustration out on your partner and kids. Go for a run before you come home, or go to yoga, or go to the gym. Then calmly share with your partner and kids what is happening to you at work, ask for their help, and ask for their comfort and support. You will draw a lot of power and encouragement from having your loving family squarely in your corner when you are back at work.

Q# 42. Does telling on a bully make me a snitch?

Is being a victim of bullying an honorable position? I don't believe that you think it is, so to answer your question I suggest that telling your organization that you are being bullied does not make you a snitch, a squealer or a complainer. Tell someone you trust about the bullying being done to you. Understand that telling on someone who is a bully is not ratting. If you do not do it for yourself, think of other people who might get hurt next.

Q# 43. What behavior or demeanor should I assume around the bully?

When you walk, look straight ahead and scan your environment, and do not hang your head or look at your feet. Feet gazing sends a message to bullies that you are fearful, while scanning the environment projects confidence and asserts that you are situationally aware. Slinking into the back of the conference room and sitting by the back wall says you are not comfortable and don't belong there. However, walking in and sitting at the table says you have purpose. Assert your physical presence. Be mindful of your body language in general, because cowering or hunched shoulders or arms wrapped around yourself (women especially) may project weakness and draw aggressive behavior from other people. Look people in the eye when you speak to them, because it projects confidence. I have witnessed a bully being put in check by a victim steadily holding his gaze and it was amazing to behold. Confidence, and a smiling demeanor, and good eye contact repels bullies. Fake it if you don't feel it to be true. Here I suggest you watch a fabulous TedTalk by Amy Cuddy, who is a social psychologist, and has researched and now practices the idea that body language affects how others see us. Her research concludes that body language may also change how we see ourselves. In the TedTalk video she displays how "power posing" - standing in a posture of confidence, even when we don't feel confident — can affect testosterone and cortisol levels in the brain, and may impact on our chances for
success. http://www.ted.com/talks/amy_cuddy_your_body_language_shapes_

Q# 44. In the face of bullying should I practice assertiveness?

As the target of bullying you must commit to learning about assertiveness and being assertive. Resentment happens when someone fails to honor a request you never actually made. Don't resent the bully if you have never told him to stop! Be direct and specific and express your needs, thoughts, and desires clearly, but without hurting anyone else. Be aware of how powerful a clear statement is to the bully, such as "...Please do not speak to me in that manner...." And then walk away. This statement may take a few times to sink in, but if you don't ask you don't get. By not objecting to how someone speaks to you when they use abusive language you are tacitly condoning their behavior and permitting them to continue. Assertiveness projects self-confidence and serves to ward away bullies. This is a skill you will need for the rest of your life, so start today and commit to expressing your wants, needs, and desires.

Q# 45. How Should I speak to a bully?

Practice what you plan to say to your bully in front of a mirror. Then when you speak to the bully, speak with a steady voice. Take a deep breath, because if your voice breaks, it sends a subliminal message that you are afraid, so breathe deeply, and speak slowly and purposely, breathing from your diaphragm. Practice deep-breathing exercises, which involve slow and deep inhalation through the nose (usually to a count of 10) followed by slow and complete exhalation for a similar count. Try this process several times a day. This breathing allows you to take normal breaths while maximizing the amount of oxygen that goes into the bloodstream, and when in a hostile situation it serves to interrupt the 'Fight or Flight' response and triggers the body's normal relaxation response.

Q# 46. Should I argue with my bully?

Nope. Nada. Never. Never argue with a bully. Don't waste your emotional energy. Bullies create conflicts to purposely upset you, so do not give him more ammunition and when in doubt refer to my pig wrestling analogy in the question above.

Q# 47. I am afraid of my bully, so how do I engage?

Fear is an emotion. Fear is induced by a threat, or a perceived threat, which causes a change in your brain and body function (think sweaty palms and armpits) and fear ultimately changes your behavior, such as freezing in the face of traumatic events, running away, hiding or avoiding. If you understand that your fear response serves as a survival mechanism, by generating appropriate behavioral responses in the face of perceived danger, then stop and examine the situation. Consciously ask yourself what is the worst thing that can happen to me? Once you realize that the worst-case scenario is the bully losing control of his emotions and screaming at you or that he will say something nasty to you or about you, but it can be ignored. Remember that his problems are his problems, so do not assume ownership of his problems, and don't make them yours. Bottom-line is that his shit is not your shit, so don't let him dump in onto you!

Q# 48. Do I need an ally when I have encountered a bully?

When you are being bullied do not allow yourself to suffer alone. Find yourself an ally and share your trauma. Don't be ashamed to tell trustworthy people what's going on. Bullying is serious and it is counterproductive to your emotional health, and to the wellbeing of the organization. You need to let people know what's happening so that they can help you. Bullies are not one-act plays. They are characters in their own mini-series, so by sharing your experiences you may discover that the bully is abusing other people too. Scratch the surface of a bullies' work life and you will find a variety of victims in various states of despair and recovery.

Q# 49. What if I plan to confront the bully?

Before you plan to confront your bully, speak to someone you trust about how you might approach the problem informally. This person could be an employee representative, a trade union official, the ombudsman or someone from HR, or even your manager or supervisor. Your manager may want to step in immediately and call the bully on his abusive behavior, however you must insist that you want to address this on your own in the first instance.

Q# 50. What should I do to avoid bullies?

You can avoid bullies by first recognizing bullying behaviors. Trust your gut. Bullies emit telltale signs and if you have been bullied before you will know what I mean. Your subconscious self can pick up on these tiny red flags, so trust your gut! Many victims of bullying will begin to tell their story by saying "…and I never saw it coming..." however when we explore the antecedence of the bullying incident or episode it usually becomes clear there were many telltale signs that the victim ignored.

Q# 51. Am I enduring workplace bullying?

To begin with, don't ignore the feeling that you are being bullied or being harassed. If you feel singled out or you are being picked on, it can be more appealing to come up with excuses for others' behavior than admit that you are being bullied. "Every new hire gets treated this way," or "I was being pompous about my new widget, so I deserved it" are common blames that we use to rationalize the bullies behavior toward us. Don't fall into a trap of self-disgust and excuse making if you feel you are being bullied. As

Sun Tsu the ancient Chinese General is reputed to have said, know your enemy and know yourself. Acknowledge the presence of the bully, and acknowledge that you are not deserving of any abusive behavior, then prepare a plan to stop the bullying and execute your plan! Reclaim your workplace, and reclaim your joy and your journey to being your highest and best self.

Q# 52. Should I tell the bully to stop?

Yes! By all means tell the bully to stop. We recognize however that this is of course, more difficult than it sounds, and I don't mean to be glib! You bought this handbook to learn how to stop the bully in your workplace, so obviously telling the bully to stop is a great first step. While you may not yet have the confidence or the assertiveness to say stop, you can keep a few simple gestures and statements in the ready to bring out when you are feeling bullied. For example, put your hands up at chest height with palms facing outwards, creating a physical barrier between you and your bully so that you can reclaim your personal space. Say something short and concise, which will communicate your frustration, such as: "Please stop and let me work" or "Stop talking please." This will help you to begin to stand up to the behavior and also give you ammunition for your report if the behavior continues.

Your first duty of care is to yourself and if you never take the step to say "stop" you are abdicating from your own responsibility to self. After you say stop then say nothing else. Do not escalate the bullying by shouting counter insults or yelling back.   This might end up getting you in trouble with the boss, or making the situation worse. Use a calm and collected tone of voice, and tell the person to stop as if you were talking to a dog chewing your shoe.

Q# 53. What should I do if I have been bullied?

Keep calm. Make sure that you have collected your evidence (the journal) and that you are calm and professional. Running to your boss in the throes of an emotional meltdown can make you seem whiny, or you are overreacting, when obviously there is a bigger issue at hand. If you remain calm, you will be more articulate, better able to present a case for yourself, and stand a better chance of changing your workplace situation. In the first instance wait overnight between a bullying episode and reporting the event to your boss. If you are re-bullied, or if you have to wait a while before talking to your boss, take efforts to avoid your bully. Take copious notes, remain calm and continue on your way.

Q# 54. Should I suggest a course of action to the boss?

After reporting bully behavior don't suggest a course of action, unless your boss requests it. Stated another way, it's inappropriate to talk to your boss about you being bullied and then to say, "Jane needs to be fired because she bullies me." Lay out your case as powerfully as possible along with all the evidence you have collected, then you can say, "I'm frustrated with this bullying behavior and I have run out of options, so I thought you needed to know." Give your supervisor the opportunity to come to their own conclusion.

Q# 55. What can I do outside of work to help myself?

In the contemporary workplace the line between our work life and our home lives have become blurred. I recommend that you create clear distinctions between your work life and home life. Engage in meaningful and fulfilling activities outside of work. You are that rare and lucky person if your work life is your passion, however for many people work is not a happy-fun-time, although the mission and the people can make the workday fulfilling. Any job, even one at a super happy and healthy workplace, can wear you down after a while and leave you in need of a vacation. Take time away from work and do something completely different, something that rejuvenates your love of work and your spirit. If you've been bullied and want to start feeling like your old self again, you should remember to reacquaint yourself with old hobbies, old friends, old and new books and movies, and of course socialize with positive friends and family.

Q# 56. Should I change jobs?

A job change is always an option. It may be that, even if the bully has been purposely dealt with, you might be more comfortable seeking new opportunities elsewhere. Even Disney characters sometimes get re-casted in happier roles. Treat your bullying experience as a learning experience rather than a setback, for it will certainly give you perspective. If you were traumatized at your place of work, maybe developing new skills in a new profession is a tonic you could use. Moving to a different environment, or just transferring to a new branch might provide you with a fresh outlook on life and work. The choice is yours as to whether you stay or go. So if you stay then stay because you made the choice to stay, not because you are trapped.

Q# 57. Should I retaliate?

In the face of bullying it may be a natural instinct to want to retaliate. Under no circumstances should you retaliate. Let me reiterate here, do not retaliate - it will throw things off balance and you could end up being blamed for being the workplace nuisance, instead of the bully. Think about the cycle of events that would unfold if you retaliated. Use the steps outlined in this handbook and the grievances processes presented by your company - but whatever you do, do not retaliate.

Q# 58. How do I ensure the bully does not get inside my head?

Most of the characters who reside in your head are there by invite only, so don't invite your bully in. Don't take what a bully says or does personally, because doing so will only damage your self-esteem. Once you take things personally the bully is now under your skin and working his way into your head and into your psyche. Carry on being yourself and carry on feeling good about yourself. Don't believe the rubbish the bully says and don't let him stop you being you. Recognize that the bully's' criticism or personal remarks are not connected to your abilities. They reflect the bully's own insecurities and weaknesses, and are meant to intimidate and control you. Stay calm, and don't be tempted to explain your behavior, because when you begin to explain your behavior you are also beginning to let the bully get into your head.

Q# 59. Is it possible to resist bullying effectively?

Resistance to bullying takes effort, however it is possible, and you will need new skills and psychological toughness. You will need to know what tactics to use. Before taking action against being bullied, you need to be prepared. This handbook offers you the material you need to begin. First you must understand what bullying is. Second, you must know how to engage a bully. Third, you must become a master observer and recorder (without emotion). Fourth, you must know how to engage your own organization, and fifth you must be prepared to engage outside help. The choice is yours.

Q# 60. How will I know when I am fully prepared to confront the bully?

Consider what resources you have at your disposal. What is your current psychological strength? Can you handle ongoing or increased incidents of bullying, and hold your head above water through a lengthy complaint process or internal struggle? How is your physical health? Can your body endure continued stress? Are you already exercising and eating well? What about money? Can you afford to lose your job or be demoted? Do you have financial reserves? Can you afford the legal expenses? Who are your allies? Are there others at work who will take your side, or who you can count on for moral support? Will your union back you? What are the state of your personal networks? Have you tended to your LinkedIn presence and your professional affiliations if you need to quickly jump ship? Do you have family and friends who will support you through the rocky times ahead? Write down a list of your resources. Conduct a SWOT analysis - your strengths, weaknesses, the perceive threat and the opportunity that will arise out of confronting your bully. Then compare the results of your SWOT to the other side's resources. Use this analysis to help decide whether to resist, to retreat or to advance. Sometimes it's better to lay low and wait until the time is right, or to let someone else take the lead. Understanding the terrain you are operating in is significant to a successful outcome.

Q# 61. How do I challenge the status quo and increase the organizations perception and outrage about mine or anothers' bullying experience?

Organizations sometimes act like sloths when presented with bullying in the workplace. The natural dynamic is to act slowly, or refuse to believe it exists, or to attribute blame to you the victim for being a nuisance, a trouble maker, or for being too sensitive. To increase outrage within the organization for your or anothers' bullying, you need to challenge the five methods (outlined above) which bullies use to diminish the significance of abusive behavior. Here's the general approach to increase outrage in your organization; (1) Expose the bullying behavior and the bully, (2) Validate your humanity and worthiness of protection by demonstrating your good performance, loyalty, honesty and other positive traits, (3) Interpret and represent the bullying as unfair, unjust and underserved, and explain why contrary explanations are wrong, (4) Mobilize support, avoid official channels or use them as tools in exposing the unfairness, (5) Refuse to be intimidated or subdued, and expose intimidation and inducement to others. I have observed that it is often difficult for a victim of bullying to advocate for themselves, so find a trusted agent who will work your outrage campaign for you, with you, or on your behalf.

Q# 62. What do I do if I am experiencing peer or horizontal bullying?

If you are experiencing peer horizontal bullying from office-mates, and you have a good relationship with your boss, then it makes sense to confide in him or her. Otherwise, the stress that is eating away at your health and productivity will seem to have no apparent cause and you really could get in trouble.

Q# 63. What do I need to understand about the culture of the organization?

Learn about the organizational culture. Review the artifacts of the organization, the mission and vision statement, the published values statement, the onboarding processes, and the company's ethics briefings. Observe what behaviors are normal, which ones are praised and which ones are stigmatized. Talk to experienced workers about how the place operates, how people get things done, and how to bring about change. You can use these insights to judge which methods are likely to win support when you report your bullying experience.

Q# 64. What is a significant first step in the face of bullying?

Acknowledge and name the abuse. Often when a target speaks to HR about their bullying problem, they're told there's nothing that can be done because no physical or illegal abuse has taken place. Naming the behaviors you are confronted with (bullying, emotional abuse) is the first step to realizing that the bullying is real and should be stopped. Understand the experience so that you can articulate the impact on the organizations' bottom-line.

Story #11.   Genie And The Jerk

Genie works for a jerk. The jerk is an excellent downward bully. Luckily she is not diminished by the bullying behavior of her boss, however she does expend an inordinate amount of time confronting him on his bad behavior, which in turn diminishes her productivity. She cannot wish his bullying out of existence! She knows there is no magic lamp that she can rub to make his horrid behavior cease, but she does own how she responds to his behavior. She acts as if he is merely sandpaper – while he scratches at and attempts to hurt her, she becomes more polished and shiny as a result.   In fact she is admired by all who encounter her for both her poise, tact and tenaciousness, in dealing with the jerk.   Genie has travelled a long road to get to this place of emotional and professional stability. She has watched the jerk devolve professionally over a number of years, and when she realized the culture of the organization was either blind to his behavior or indifferent, she accepted that she had to manage the situation herself.   Emotions can be contagious, so Genie does not allow herself to be contaminated by the negative bully behaviors, rather she exudes a happy and positive disposition in the face of bullying and hostility.   Genie has internalized the belief that it is possible to intentionally and thoughtfully control and change her own emotional state. Her operating model is that her bosses' BS is not her BS – while it is a problem, she refuses to allow it to become her problem.   Genie serves as an inspiration to many of us.

Section 7: What Is So Important About The Journal?

Q# 65. Should I journal in a bullying workplace, even if I don't believe I am being bullied myself?

Even if you are not sure you are being bullied, journaling about your feelings, experiences, and emotions, may help you to explore and figure out for yourself what you are struggling with. As a result of writing down and reflecting upon your feelings you will have created an understanding of your situation.

Q# 66. If I am being bullied what should I journal about?

Keep a record of all bullying events. Record the name of your bully instigator and the method of bullying. Be as specific as possible; Record times, dates, locations, and the names of any observer to the events. Provide and gather as much information as you can. Collecting documentation is the most important and certain way to get the bullying to stop when you take the issue higher up the organizational chain, or to an external legal team.

Q# 67. Should I document every encounter with the bully?

Yes! Document and keep records of all encounters, meetings and conversations you have with the bully, including date, time and place with a short description of all events, and all detail no matter how small. Note that making a recording without consent of the other person is often problematic, so be wary of your state laws on this matter. Also, making covert recordings is a violation of trust, so only choose this path if the association is beyond repair and the bully instigator's actions are extreme. (Note too that some organizations have expressly prohibited the presence of a recording device in their workspace, so don't let this be a reason for the organization to fire you).

Q# 68. What are the foundations of a well written diary or journal?

There are two purposes to your journal. The first purpose serves to document the bullying and unwelcomed experience, and the second purpose serves to prepare to communicate the experience to a third party - so write with the audience in mind. Documentation is the most certain process to demonstrate the intent behind the bully instigators' behavior. On the topic of documentation you will also need evidence about what has happened, good enough to convince a disbeliever. Therefore, the foundation of a good journal will include regular entries describing what happens during each encounter: For example, "At 8am I put my file on Jim's desk. At 9am. Jim stormed into my office, threw the file in my trash can, scowled and shouted that "This is crap", and left before I had a chance to respond".

Remember to frequently record exact quotes in your journal. Consistency of documentation looks for patterns of note taking, so even if what the bully said was not deeply egregious be sure to quote him. This pays dividends later when you quote truly egregious statements, as you have demonstrated a consistent approach to recording exact quotes. To augment your diary, which is a personal account - thus subject to bias - you need to collect backup material. Letters, handwritten notes, or emails are very helpful. So too are statements from others. For example, if there is an encounter or a meeting and the bully instigator makes a snide comment whenever you speak, write a short account and ask a witness to sign it. They may not be comfortable in signing such a statement, so in lieu of their signature make a note that you requested their signature and they declined. This brings up the issue of building support. If you have some observers who can and will corroborate the abuse, you are in a much stronger position. But be wary of whose support you elicit. In a toxic organization where bullying is the cultural norm (or tacitly condoned), there are the usual sycophants who will use your harm to their advantage, so don't be naive. Some observers may say they will support you, but then tell the bully instigator about your journaling for their own benefit, and undermine you by exposing your vulnerabilities. Talk to a trusted peer first about your experiences. If she says "...I saw how the boss responded abusively towards you during Monday's meeting, do you know that that is considered downward bullying?" you could ask if she is willing to confirm that in writing. You should already have the write-up in your journal so you can easily e-mail her with the details that you have recorded and ask her to confirm your understanding of the experience.

Eventually you will have recorded a series of incidents that will represent a systematic bullying experience, and you will have backup documentation to support each incident. Here you will have to take the initiative and write an executive summary, to make ease of reading for the first series of reviewers of your complaint. Make it simple. Just state the facts in chronological order. Start with a single statement of the issue and keep it succinct. Keep the summary to less than one page. If you are not a strong writer, ask a trusted friend for help to improve the clarity of your summary.

With your summary organized and even indexed and tabbed with supporting documentation, you now have the first elements of your case against the instigator bully. Proceed carefully though, because this experience has happened to you and you are raw. Others might see your emotionally impacted self and wonder if you are not the one with the problem. Seek out a party who's not directly involved with the bully, preferably someone who is two levels above him and formally request a meeting. Present your executive summary, journal and attachments, and state that you are here formally to address a case of bullying.

Q# 69. Should I document the bully's behavior towards and around me?

The short answer is document everything. Every time a bullying incident happens write down the WHO, WHAT, WHEN, WHERE and WHY. Also keep any bullying emails or other tangible documents. (For the long answer on how to document see above.)

Q# 70. What does it mean when someone tells me too document the bully's behavior?

Keep track of the problem. The first practical step is one many targets of bullying overlook, which is to document the incident. As a bullied target you must document your bullying experience as soon as possible so that you do not forget key information. The added advantage of documentation is that the experience this will help you to regain control over the situation.

Q# 71. Should I keep notes on the bully's behavior towards me?

Keep a journal. (See answer above). To assist in dealing with the traumatic event and to prevent you from feeling depressed, write your feelings and thoughts in a journal. The experience is cathartic, and even if you have never kept a journal before this experience will prove very worthwhile. Keep your journal safe and away from prying eyes. If you use your work computer to record your experiences please be sure to store the document so that no one can easily open it. However, remember that in most jurisdictions all data on your work computer is discoverable and your employer can have access to it on demand. As a backup measure either print off and take home, or e-mail your files to a personal address. As a practical matter if you were terminated you will have a very difficult time getting access to personal information stored in your work space or on your work computer, so keep backup files at home.

Q# 72. Should my journal include an acknowledgement of my emotional state?

Acknowledge your emotions, but do not write emotionally. This is an important distinction, when documenting an instance of bullying, just stick to the facts, and not over emphasize your emotional responses. This is not easy, however you must understand the future readers' perspective when they read the babblings of an incoherent victim of bullying, and wonder if you are perhaps the problem, rather than the accused bully instigator.

Q# 73. How do I accurately record a bullying incident if I am away from my desk?

Always keep a small notepad with you so you don't have to rely on your memory. You will look very attentive as you take notes during the ass-chewing or other bullying behavior or verbal abuse being hurled at you, and this way you will have a real-time record of what was said to you. Or you can use the recording device on your mobile phone!!!

Q# 74. Should I keep a list of bullying incident observers?

The best case for a bullying defense is one that includes being observed by a third party. Consult with your fellow co-workers any time you feel you have been bullied and make sure they'll back you up by corroborating your journal entry. Have them write it down for future reference. Even if they won't write it down send them a copy of your observations and ask them to confirm it. Pick someone who works the same shift as you do, or who has a desk near yours. If bullying tends to happen at particular times or in particular locations, have your witness linger in the area where you suspect you are going to be tormented by your bully. Bring allies into a meeting with a superior who you feel bullies you. You'll have backup in case things get ugly and you'll have evidence for later.

Q# 75. What is the point of keeping a diary?

In a case against a bully, the diary is known as a contemporaneous record. It will be very useful and valuable if you decide to take action against your bully at a later stage.

Section 8: What Do I Need To Know To Make A Formal Complaint?

Q# 76. What am I going to do with the documentation once I have collected and recorded sufficient information?

Hopefully you have followed the path outlined to effective documentation and it now reflects a pattern of intentional, destructive, abusive, hostile and bullying behavior.   Your organization really has no choice but to respond to the allegation. Your initial contact is with the Human Resources (HR) representative, and you must share your detailed documentation with them. Don't make assessments about their neutrality in this situation, just provide them with a copy of the information (not your only copy of course).   You must go on record with the HR office and give them the opportunity to accept your complaint file and review its contents.   You want your abusive situation to be taken seriously, so you have to have the courage to complain to HR.   You may not trust them but they are the step you cannot afford to miss…so give them a chance to be on your side from the very beginning.

Q# 77. Should I be concerned about the organizational cost of bullying behavior towards me?

Try to determine cost of the bullying. Managers will respond to a business case for ending bullying more so than they will respond to personal or emotional complaints such as, "I'm hurting, can you help me?" Quantify the damage as best you can, and your manager will be more responsive.

Q# 78. What do I do if my initial attempts at presenting a complaint don't work?

If your initial attempts aren't working, it's worth stepping up your game to get a result. Move your issue higher up the chain. Talk to a person in higher authority and let them take responsibility for resolving the matter. Employers have a legal duty to stop bullying, and you have rights as an employee to file a complaint and be heard. Usually you can be heard through a formal complaints procedure, or even at an industrial tribunal or court.

Q# 79. How should I approach the HR office?

Schedule a formal meeting with your supervisor and/or just the HR representative. Bring your written evidence, your witnesses, and present your case as calmly as you can. Practice what you are planning to say before you get in there then say it. Keep your complaint short and to the point, and fill out any documentation or paperwork provided to you by the HR officer.

Q# 80. What if after I told my boss about the bulling nothing changes?

Follow up. If the bullying continues or it still hasn't been sorted out and nothing is being done to stop it, you have the right to take it further and go higher up in the organization, by talking to higher management personnel and even to HR. Continue until your complaint is taken seriously and the situation is remedied. You are entitled to work in a safe and bully free environment.

Q# 81. Should I make a formal complaint?

Yes. If you are being bullied at work and you are undermined, humiliated, denigrated, shouted at, or isolated, then you are being bullied and you should make a complaint about the impact of this behavior on your ability to perform your job.

Q# 82. Should I be skeptical of official channels?

Yes, experience has shown that victims of bullying should be skeptical of official channels, as all persons in those channels are not as equally committed to understanding and stamping out the phenomenon of workplace bullying. It is tempting to seek help by using formal processes, for example reporting the matter to the boss's boss or to the board of management, or making a complaint using an internal grievance procedure, or making a submission to a review panel. Unfortunately, these channels seldom offer the respite you need in the short-term and can even make matters worse. Don't put all your eggs in the 'official channels' basket – take ownership of the bullying problem and assume the courage to confront your bully.

Q# 83. How do some organizations respond differently to the allegations of bullying?

In some institutions and companies, the people higher up in the organization nearly always support the chain of command. A top manager will almost always support subordinates in the face of initial challenges from lower-level employees. Be aware of the inherent need that senior managers have to trust and support their next-in-line subordinates. If you are the only complainer there is no trend data to support the complaint so the senior manager does not see this situation as a problem for the organization. However, if there are several discrete complaints against the manager from different sources, then the senior leaders will begin to recognize that there is a problem.

Q# 84. What are the disadvantages of following a formal grievance procedure?

Grievance procedures are notoriously slow, and it could take months for your complaint to be dealt with, meanwhile the bullying continues or you are left in limbo. Procedurally, the focus of the complaints process is on technicalities, not the unfairness of the behavior, such as; did you complain within the appropriate time frame; did you complain in the right manner; did you meet the expectations of the complaint process. In the experience of many people who were bullied they have concluded that the grievance process is not intended to protect the employee, rather it is designed to protect the employer. If a case were to go to trial and the judges asked the employer what procedures did they have in place, the company is in the clear. The company can honestly state that they have a formal complaint process, albeit ineffective in terms of resolving your situation.

Complaint processes and grievance procedures are also time-consuming - you end up spending vast amounts of time and effort preparing submissions and responding to queries. A skeptic would begin to think that the process is purposely onerous to dissuade victims of bullying from filing a grievance. Pursuing a grievance can be expensive – especially if you need legal assistance to make your case. Grievance processes are fraught with lack of transparency. Understandably many matters are handled without publicity, and often confidentiality is expected. This serves as a form of cover-up. Unfortunately this is a double edged sword, as the presence of interviewers or investigators in your workplace, whose purpose is unexplained yet very obvious, only serves to add fuel to an otherwise volatile situation.

Experienced victims of bullying will tell you that unless you have allies in high places, using official channels is probably a bad idea. It will give people the impression that the matter is being handled appropriately, when in fact this is just a charade. Victims of bullying who have engaged a formal grievance process will tell you that the only winner in the entire process was their attorney, who was paid for their effort. Experience has shown many bully victims that the formal grievance process puts them at a long-term disadvantage. Instead, they should either run dual strategies or just focus on mobilizing support, namely getting others to understand what's happened and then to take action against the bullying directly.

Section 9: What Do I Do In The Face Of Organizational Non-Responsiveness?

Q# 85. What do I do if the culture of the organization condones bullying?

If a bullying culture is ingrained in the company, the best option may be to move on and find a company with a healthier culture.

Q# 86. If I am being bullied should I look for a new job?

There are many jobs out there. If you are being bullied and things get out of control, find another job. It is not the end of the world to search for another job. If you are afraid you will not get any recommendations or references and this is why you are staying, it means you are being blackmailed to stay. Do not give away your power to vote with your feet. Chances are you will not get good recommendations anyway, so rip off the bandage and go out into the world. Be confident in saying that the culture of the organization you just departed did not match your values.

Q# 87. Should I prepare a list of acceptable alternative realities?

It would be helpful to come up with a variety of alternatives to help make the situation better for you. If your bully boss's supervisor is unwilling to fire your boss but acknowledges that bullying has occurred, are you willing to transfer within the organization? Are you willing to work from home? What would make the situation "right" by you? Give each alternative some serious thought in case you need to quickly present a case for yourself. Understand what alternative realities you can live with.

Q# 88. How do I know if my organization condones the bully's behavior?

You can achieve valuable insight by examining the tactics employed by the organization in response to other sorts of injustices in your organization. For example, explore how the company addressees unfair evaluations, workplace violence, sexual harassment, or ageism or sexism?

Q# 89. My boss condones bullying - what can I do?

My boss is a bully enabler. He permits inappropriate conduct to occur in meetings – he allows the office bully to constantly interrupt and prevent others from speaking. The boss acts as a go-between when the bully refuses to interact with other people on the team who he thinks are incapable of understanding his brilliance.   What can I do? The answer is that we must recognize that failure of leadership is invariably behind the rise of bullying in organizations.   It is not your responsibility to train your leader to be a leader, however we all must learn to manage our boss. After the staff meeting you can express your concern to your boss…"Jim, I am aware that our meetings with you could be more productive if Jack did not keep interrupting us – can you help us by asking Jack to cut it out…".   There is nothing to be lost by asking your boss to be the leader he is supposed to be, but do it in a respectful manner.

Q# 90. Is there any reason an organization should allow bullying to endure?

A bullying culture is bad for business. There is absolutely no logical or sane excuse why bullying behavior should be allowed to continue in an organization, however organizations do not always understand the impact or accept the liability associated with the presence of bullying behavior.

Q# 91. What do I do if the company I work for condones bullying?

If you are working in a company that rewards bullying behavior, you would be better served to jump ship and watch your now-former company's inevitable demise from the safety of your new job. Even if you have no job to go to it is not in your interest to stay where you are at. Although no one should ever be in this position, when your physical health, sanity, and happiness hang in the balance, I totally understand why making that move is the right decision. Many victims are handcuffed to retirement schemes and face the prospect of losing it all if they leave the company. The worst case however is to remain in a situation that is causing your physical and mental health to deteriorate, making you less employable when you finally are ready to leave the company.

Section 10: Should I Seek Outside Help?

Q# 92. Should I speak to an attorney?

If you present evidence to your company and nothing changes or the situation becomes worse, consult an attorney and consider legal action. Provide them with documentation and seek to pursue legal action. Speak to an attorney if management doesn't help you handle the issue or the bullying continues. It is neither fair nor appropriate for you to live in fear of your workplace or feel that your safety or quality of life is being compromised by a bully. Initial consultations with personal injury attorneys are typically free. The attorney can advise you on what to do next. Be wary though that an attorney will only take a case if he sees that he will get paid – either in settlement or through paying his hourly rate, which is not cheap.

Q# 93. Should I look outside the organization for support?

Yes, look outside the workplace for moral, physical, and emotional support. Be sure to seek support from family, friends, and professionals such as a doctor, counselor, coach, mentor or your spiritual leader. One of the bully's strategies is to purposefully make the target feel isolated, anxious, depressed and helpless. Take stock of your outside resources and call upon them for help and support.

Q# 94. Should I seek professional help?

If things are really bad don't be afraid to go to your doctor and take time off sick or use some annual leave. Talk to your mental health provider. You might be in need of more substantial care than you can provide by yourself. Therapy or medication might be in order if you've spent a considerable amount of time in the grip of a workplace bully.

Q# 95. Should I ask my mentor for help?

Be aware that if your bully is above you on the organization chart you will need a mentor equal or greater in stature to the bully to be of assistance. The company's internal mentorship program is not usually intended to address issues of bullying, however a mentor may have a broader perspective, and can help you navigate through the bullying experience and the grievance processes within the organization.

Q# 96. Should I engage my executive coach to help me navigate through

the bullying experience?

I am clearly biased when I answer this question (as I am an executive coach) but I would completely agree with employing your coach to help you navigate through this bullying experience. Here is what you can accomplish with your executive coach. A coach will help you to become a more skillful observer of yourself and remind you of some basic truths;

- Pain is inevitable, however suffering is optional. Your coach will help you navigate to a different interpretation of the workplace story you are currently experiencing.

- Attachment is the root of pain and suffering.   Your coach can help you to detach from the experience of being bullied.

- If you want to create a new reality, then at some point you have to declare the future. Your coach will hold you accountable to achieve this future reality.

Section 11: What Should I Do As A Leader In The Organization?

Story #12.   The Power Of Feedback

During my last assignment I had the opportunity to participate in a 360 degree review process. I had a great team and I was very proud of our accomplishments. I have learned not to fear feedback and appreciate it for the gift it is intended to be. I encouraged my team to be forthright in completing the feedback instrument, as I valued their perspective and I know I am still learning about being and remaining the best leader I can be. During the one-on-one feedback session with the coach I was surprised to learn about how my team felt I had behaved during a certain period of our project development phase. Apparently I had reverted back to an earlier and less user-friendly version of myself during a period of high-stress. I was not unfamiliar with this aspect of my leadership style and had gone to great lengths to keep this aspect in check. Apparently however I permitted this deviant behavior to reenter my work life during a period of high stress – as stress was averring both in my work life and my personal life. While I was not proud of this behavior I was deeply appreciative that my team took the effort to bring this recurring deviant behavior to my awareness. I remember thinking how proud I was of my team that they trusted me enough to bring this information forward during a 360 review. How courageous of them.   I was so prideful that I almost missed the teaching point here…. Why if I was acting like a jerk had my guys not told me immediately when the behavior happened. Had I not created a sufficiently open and honest and engaging culture that my team would be unafraid to tell me when I was acting like a jerk? The question I now ponder is the apparent disconnect between my espoused behavior and my actual behavior in the workplace. Self-reflection needs to be a daily activity.

Q# 97. Is it possible that I am part of the problem?

How can you tell whether you are part of the bullying problem in your organization? You can ask a neutral party - but remember, if you typically react badly to negative feedback, others won't want to tell you the truth. Here are some questions you can pose and answer for yourself (1) Have I had conflicts with several different people inside and outside my organization (2) Have I been hiding or withholding any information - is my leadership style transparent? (3) Do I resist opportunities to openly discuss difficult organizational issues? (4) Do I make disparaging comments about others, openly or while gossiping - even in jest? (5) Have I threatened anyone in my organization, either personally or professionally? Depending upon how honestly you answer these questions will provide you an insight to how and if you contribute to the bullying culture in your own organization.

Q# 98. As an employer how do I begin a bullying prevention program?

Begin by formally announcing and implementing a zero-tolerance bullying policy at your business. Also, be sure that any existing health and wellness policies include anti-bullying protocols. Make sure this bully-prevention initiative is more than just an exercise, that it is supported by management at all levels, and is taken seriously at all levels of the company.

Q# 99. As a leader what should I do?

Address bullying behaviors immediately. Work can be stress-free if you choose to sit back and hope for the best; however, imaginary thinking about your employees being able to work it out among themselves is a failure of leadership. It won't work and they won't sort it out without intervention. Don't let a bullying problem fester among your employees if you want a productive, healthy, and effective work environment.

Q# 100.   Should I investigate all bullying complaints?

While it is not always possible to investigate all complaints yourself, ensure that each complaint is reviewed fully and taken seriously. Even if complaints seem frivolous or appear to frequently come from overly sensitive employees, which then turn out to be merely simple misunderstandings, they are worthy of your attention and this lets all of your employees know that the organization is committed to resolving claims of abuse and injustice.

Q# 101.   What should I do about individual or unit competition in my organization?

If you want to eliminate abusive behavior and bullying then you will also have to eliminate competition in your organization. Often workplace bullying evolves from a sense of competition in the workplace, leading employees who feel threatened by the skills or accomplishments of other employees to become a bully. Or employees are abused by attempts to bring them down or sabotage their work effort. Bullies will use the cover of the competitive process to engage in psychological warfare against other employees. Competition contributes to a dangerous and problematic workplace dynamic. Workplace competition between individuals and units is predicated upon the belief that employees want to perform at their best and will work harder when rewarded for their successes. While it is true that competition in some business models can increase productivity and output, the same type of culture can also increase employee turnover and create a hostile work environment.

Q# 102.   As a leader what can I do to deter bullying in my organization?

As a leader you should encourage management and staff interaction throughout the organization. The more involved your workforce is at all levels, the less likely are managers to bully subordinates, and the less likely are the lower level employees to take matters into their own hands when confronted with a bullying situation.

Q# 103.   As a leader, how should I deal with a bullying situation when it is reported to me?

As a leader you have both a moral and legal duty to act if bullying is reported to you in the workplace, or in some instances when the bullying occurs between employees outside of the workplace. Make sure you understand and follow your company's policy when dealing with bullying behaviors. And regardless of the gravity of the bullying, you need the target (victim) to remain involved and understand that they are in control of the situation. Ask the target how they want the matter to be resolved, and if they are unsure, offer them some options and let them choose. For example, if you go headlong into a confrontation with the bully, this may make things worse for the victim in the long-run. An alternative approach would be to offer assertiveness training to the target and to coach them through addressing the behavior directly with the bully themselves. Basically, your job as a leader and manager is to do what is right by the victim,

Q# 104.   As a leader in my organization what can I do to prevent

bullying?

Develop a company policy related to bullying and bullying prevention. Within the policy you should define what bullying is, and provide examples of unacceptable behavior (this handbook will serve as a good source for information about what bullying is). Show support for employees by assuring them it is their right to work in an anti-bullying environment. Provide clear instructions to employees for how to manage and report abusive workplace behaviors.

Q# 105.   How do I deal with a bullying situation if I see it happening to someone else?

If you see it happening in your domain, you must have the courage to address it head on.   Pull the bully aside and let him know that you witnessed his abusive behavior. Cut it off at the knees and leave him with the full understanding that you will not tolerate this type of behavior in your organization. Furthermore, as a leader your alarm bells should ring loudly in your ears if a colleague or a subordinates' behavior changes drastically, e.g. unexplained drop in performance, inability to concentrate, loss of confidence, withdrawal, using drink or drugs to get by, or difficulties sleeping. As suggested elsewhere in this handbook, that notwithstanding the hazard of attempting to turn leaders into amateur psychologists, interpersonal understanding of the complexities of the human dynamic will help you establish the framework and language for a constructive work environment. For example, an adept and insightful manager may discern that the above changes in a colleague or employee is an indicator of some underlying problem. Don't approach the issue head-on, maybe go for a coffee together and say you've noticed something's up, and encourage them to talk. You never know, it may be just the neighbors' baby's teething problems keeping them awake at night! Or maybe a bully has struck in the heart of your organization and your colleague or subordinate is too ashamed to talk about it.

Q# 106.   How should I behave towards a colleague if they are being bullied?

If you know that your colleague is experiencing abusive workplace behavior, the most important thing you can do is listen carefully, and offer practical advice such as writing a diary detailing where and when the bullying behavior happens. Remind your colleague that recording events in a diary has two benefits; writing things down factually gives your colleague much needed emotional distance from the event, and the diary can also support a formal proceeding against the bully.   Resist the temptation to get angry at the bully, as this only adds to your colleagues' emotional burden, not lessen it.

Q# 107.   Should I help my colleague or peer to defend themselves?

Help your colleague by helping them prepare a plan of attack. Maybe you could act as an ally in meetings, if that is when the bully most often strikes. A bully will desist if he sees that your colleague is not alone and has strong support from other colleagues.

Q# 108.   What is my responsibility towards bullying in the organization?

Whether you are the target, the perpetrator or an observer of bullying and abusive behavior, you have responsibility to become part of the solution. Abstaining from becoming involved only makes you part of the problem.

Q# 109.   As a leader what do I need to know about the organizational costs of bullying?

Specifically, you need to know about the cost of dealing with high attrition, constant employee turnover, inability to attract top talent to your organization, increased healthcare costs, poor employee morale (which impacts customer service and product quality), potential lawsuits, rampant absenteeism, and costs of re-training.

Story #13.   Humor Among Colleagues

John – I noticed that you used self-effacing humor today during our staff meeting to alleviate the tension when we were discussing the upcoming reorganization. I applaud and thank you for the intervention. I do want to bring to your attention however that while you also included Will in your humor he did not appear to appreciate you poking fun at him too. I believe you hurt his feelings.   I am curious as to why you chose to direct your humor at Will as well? I felt that the situation was uncomfortable for Will. What was your take on the conversation?

Answer A: "Geeze Tina – I think you are being overly sensitive here – Will and I have worked together for years – everyone knows that we banter back and forth – I don't see how it was a problem. OK John, as your boss I am telling you it was a problem today and I am asking you to be more aware of your interactions with Will, especially in front of our younger and more impressionable staff."

Answer B: " You know Tina, I would be horrified if I had offended Will today-we have been colleagues for many years! Thanks for the feedback! Let me go over and check in with him and make sure we are ok!"

Section 12 - Top Ten Things For Leaders To Do To Promote A Non-Bullying Culture In The Work Place

Leaders and managers are the first line of defense in preventing workplace bullying and incivility in the organization. My gift to you in this section are my personal leadership strategies towards creating a civil and zero-bullying workplace.   I fully recognize how the impact and stressors of our daily lives can derail our commitment towards becoming our highest and best selves and creating the best organizations. As a leader, the act of recognizing and aspiring to be more civil in the workplace is your first step toward creating a non-bullying environment.   And as a leader myself, my job is to ensure that you have the tools to succeed and to achieve your goals. This final section is my way of reinforcing my commitment to you as you move forward on your journey towards creating a civil and bully-free work place. As a leader (regardless of where you sit in the organization);

1. Applaud and acknowledge civil behavior in others. Train your team by expressing a zero-policy towards bullying and endorsing civil behavior.

2. Becoming situationally aware by soliciting anonymous feedback, and investigating professional and personal dissonance, especially regarding top performers.

3. Model civil behavior. Leaders must take the lead in shaping employees attitude regarding bullying behaviors and incivility.

4. Rebuke uncivil and bully behavior in others. Rebuke uncivil behavior in others civilly. (No point in being a jerk about telling a jerk that he is a jerk).

5. Reflect upon your own behavior regularly – are you the cause of bully behaviors in your organization. Treat others as you would want to be treated.

6. Train yourself in creating an awareness of and recognizing destructive emotions as they occur in others, such as envy and jealousy, and the concept of retaliation and revenge.

7. Train yourself to be cognizant of how employees' personality traits affect both job performance, and perception of bullying and incivility.

8. Train to enhance your team's awareness by exploring bullying, uncivil and rude and disrespectful behavior.

9. Train, Teach, Coach and Mentor other managers and leaders to moderate their own behavior!

10. Weed out bully behaviors and incivility through effective hiring – be quick to "fix" bad hiring decisions.

Did You Like This Hand Book?

Before you go I'd like to say "thanks" for purchasing this handbook. I am of the belief that a harmonious and civil workplace is the underpinning of healthy and prosperous organizations, communities and our democratic society. My life as a leader is framed in the belief that there are no scoundrels, merely workers who are hurting or have been hurt, who have experienced perceived or actual injustice, or who are confident and comfortable in their ignorance. The bully in the workplace is frequently a coward, who has been hurt or is hurting, who believes he has experienced injustice, or is confident and comfortable in his ignorance and baseness. This handbook is not intended to fix the bully - this handbook is intended to stop his behavior, to save the employee from more harm, and to improve the culture and health of the organization. Perhaps at another time I will write a book on how to save the bully, but not today!

If you gleaned any new insights from this book, or experienced an ah-ha moment I would appreciate your positive feedback on the Amazon website. I strive to provide effective learning insights to you as my clients and customers, and your positive feedback reinforces both my approach and my business.

Notes

Allen, B. A. (2005). A springboard for building a more respectful workplace.

Altmiller, G. M. (2008). Incivility in nursing education: Student perceptions. Available from ProQuest Dissertations and Theses database. (UMI No. 3313308)

Andersson, L. M., & Pearson, C. M. (1999). Tit for tat? The spiraling effect of incivility in the workplace. The Academy of Management. Academy of Management Review, 24(3), 452-471. doi:10. 2307/259136

Aquino, K., Tripp, T. M., & Bies, R. J. (2006). Getting even or moving on? Power, procedural justice, and types of offense as predictors of revenge, forgiveness, reconciliation, and avoidance in organizations. Journal of Applied Psychology, 91(3), 653-658. doi:10. 1037/0021-9010. 91. 3. 653

Bame, R. M. (2013). A historical study on workplace bullying. (Order No. 3585973, University of Phoenix). ProQuest Dissertations and Theses, , 162. Retrieved from http://search.proquest.com/docview/1511999866?accountid=35812. (1511999866).

Bandow, D., & Hunter, D. (2007). The rise of workplace incivilities: Has it happened to you? The Business Review, Cambridge, 7(1), 212-217. Retrieved from http://search. proquest. com. ezproxy. apollolibrary. com/docview/197302201?accountid=35812

Baruch, Y., & Jenkins, S. (2006). Swearing at work and permissive leadership culture: When antisocial becomes social and incivility was acceptable. Leadership and Organization Development Journal, 28(6), 492-507. doi:10. 1108/01437730710780958

Beaudette, J. (2012). Backstabbing bosses and callous co-workers: A mixed methods examination of the experience of working with a psychopath. (Order No. MR93530, Carleton University (Canada)). ProQuest Dissertations and Theses, , 165. Retrieved from http://search.proquest.com/docview/1365811996?accountid=35812. (1365811996).

Benson, W. L. (2013). Workplace psychological aggression: Resolving the battle of competing constructs. (Order No. 3587053, Washington State University). ProQuest Dissertations and Theses, , 121. Retrieved from http://search.proquest.com/docview/1426811098?accountid=35812. (1426811098).

Birney, L. L. (2004). Trust and bullying: Antagonistic forces. (Order No. 3151687, The University of Texas at San Antonio). ProQuest Dissertations and Theses, , 208-208 p. Retrieved from http://search.proquest.com/docview/305050694?accountid=35812. (305050694).

Blackstock, S. (2012). Addressing quality of worklife: Examining horizontal workplace bullying behaviors in nursing. (Order No. MR87526, University of Northern British Columbia (Canada)). ProQuest Dissertations and Theses, , 108. Retrieved from http://search.proquest.com/docview/1026756811?accountid=35812. (1026756811).

Bolman, L. G., & Deal, T. E. (2008). Reframing organizations: Artistry, choice, and leadership (4th ed.). San Francisco, CA: Jossey-Bass.

Bowditch, J. L., Buono A. F., & Stewart M. M. (2008). A primer on organizational behavior (7th ed.). Hoboken, NJ. John Wiley & Sons Inc.

Bowling, N. A., & Eschleman, K. J. (2010). Employee personality as a moderator of the relationships between work stressors and counterproductive work behavior. Journal of Occupational Health Psychology, 15(1), 91-103. doi:10. 1037/a0017326

Bowling, N. A., & Gruys, M. L. (2010). Overlooked issues in the conceptualization and measurement of counterproductive work behavior. Human Resource Management Review, 20(1), 54-61. doi:10. 1016/j. hrmr. 2009. 03. 008

Brannan, S. A. (2006). An organizational culture perspective of individual experiences of covert and/or indirect aggression in organizations: A grounded theory study. (Order No. 3274164, Gonzaga University). ProQuest Dissertations and Theses, , 357. Retrieved from http://search.proquest.com/docview/304948329?accountid=35812. (304948329).

Burrill, K. A. (2006). Bully victimization, PTSD risk factors and dissociation: A correlational study. (Order No. 3218098, Union Institute and University). ProQuest Dissertations and Theses, , 84-84 p. Retrieved from http://search.proquest.com/docview/304913614?accountid=35812. (304913614).

Cabrera, C. M. (2012). Relationship of teachers' perceptions of organizational health and work-place bullying. (Order No. 3515793, Fairleigh Dickinson University). ProQuest Dissertations and Theses, , 72. Retrieved from http://search.proquest.com/docview/1027902305?accountid=35812. (1027902305).

Campana, K. L. (2009). Leader incivility and its effect on group processes and performance. Available from ProQuest Dissertations and Theses database. (UMI No. 3387250)

Carlock, D. H. (2013). Beyond bullying: A holistic exploration of the organizational toxicity phenomenon. (Order No. 3556871, Pepperdine University). ProQuest Dissertations and Theses, , 181. Retrieved from http://search.proquest.com/docview/1328403875?accountid=35812. (1328403875).

Carroll-Garrison, M. (2007). Efficacy of the U. S. quest for global democratization in a non-secular world (Unpublished master's thesis). Excelsior College, New York.

Carroll-Garrison, M. (2012). An exploration of managers' awareness and reaction to workplace incivility: A grounded theory study. (Order No. 3532732, University of Phoenix). ProQuest Dissertations and Theses , 285. Retrieved from http://search.proquest.com/docview/1222928827? accountid=35812. (1222928827).

Carroll-Garrison, M. (2014). Workplace Incivility Is Bad For Business: What Managers Need to Know Toward Eradicating Incivility, Creating a Civil Workplace, and Improving the Bottom Line. Scholars' Press.

Carter, S. T. (1998). Civility: Manners, morals, and the etiquette of democracy. New York, NY:

Harper Perennial. 5

Cortina, L. M. (2008). Unseen injustice: Incivility as modern discrimination in organizations. Academy of Management Review, 33(1), 55-75. doi:10. 5465/AMR. 2008. 27745097

Cortina, L. M., & Magley, V. J. (2009). Patterns and profiles of response to incivility in the workplace. Journal of Occupational Health Psychology, 14(3), 272-288. doi:10. 1037/a0014934

Cortina, L. M., Magley, V. J., Williams, J. H., & Langhout, R. D. (2001). Incivility in the workplace: Incidence and impact. Journal of Occupational Health Psychology, 6(1), 64-80. doi:10. 1037/1076-8998. 6. 1. 64

Cowan, R. L. (2009). Walking the tightrope: Workplace bullying and the human resource professional. (Order No. 3400699, Texas A&M University). ProQuest Dissertations and Theses, , 277-n/a. Retrieved from http://search.proquest.com/docview/305116539?accountid=35812. (305116539).

Crampton, S. M., & Hodge, J. W. (2008). Rudeness and incivility in the workplace. Journal of Leadership Accountability and Ethics, 8, 41-48. Retrieved from http://search. proquest. com. ezproxy. apollolibrary. com/docview/197584978?accountid=35812

Daft, R. L., & Marcic, C. (2008). Understanding Management (7th ed.). Mason, OH: South-Western Cengage Learning.

Daniel, B. (2004). Workplace bullying: A communication perspective. (Order No. 3156069, The Florida State University). ProQuest Dissertations and Theses, , 189-189 p. Retrieved from http://search.proquest.com/docview/305184638?accountid=35812. (305184638).

Daniel, T. A. (2009). "Tough boss" or workplace bully?: A grounded theory study of insights from human resource professionals. (Order No. 3350585, Fielding Graduate University). ProQuest Dissertations and Theses, , 277-n/a. Retrieved from http://search.proquest.com/docview/305169091? accountid=35812. (305169091).

De Pedro, M. M., Sánchez, M. I., Navarro, M. C., & Izquierdo, M. G. (2008). Workplace mobbing and effects on workers' health. Spanish Journal of Psychology, 11(1), 219-227. Retrieved from http://search. proquest. com. ezproxy. apollolibrary. com/docview/274715425?accountid=35812

Denton, L. T., & Campbell, C. (2009). Dementors in our midst: Managing the highly productive but morale-killing employee. Journal of Applied Management and Entrepreneurship, 14(1), 3-25. Retrieved from http://search. proquest. com. ezproxy. apollolibrary. com/docview/203914081? accountid=35812

Derrer, R. D. (2005). The ontological status of bullies and victims. (Order No. 3204707, Michigan State University). ProQuest Dissertations and Theses, , 76-76 p. Retrieved from http://search.proquest.com/docview/305428306?accountid=35812. (305428306).

Dickinson, L. A. (2013). Witness responses to workplace horizontal bullying. (Order No. 3572570, Seattle University). ProQuest Dissertations and Theses, , 248. Retrieved from http://search.proquest.com/docview/1433290619?accountid=35812. (1433290619).

Duff, A.J. (2013). The Effect Of Work Shame On Innovative Behavior: A Multi-Source Field Study

Eastman, G. B. (2013). The relationship between psychological capital and workplace bullying for nurses. (Order No. 3575191, Northcentral University). ProQuest Dissertations and Theses, , 141. Retrieved from http://search.proquest.com/docview/1459811462?accountid=35812. (1459811462).

Estes, B., & Wang, J. (2008). Integrative literature review: Workplace incivility: Effects on individual and organizational performance. Human Resource Management Review, 7(2), 218-240. doi:10. 1177/1534484308315565

Everton, W. J., Jolton, J. A., & Mastrangelo, P. M. (2007). Be nice and fair or else: Understanding reasons for employees' deviant behaviors. The Journal of Management Development, 26(2), 117-131. doi:10. 1108/02621710710726035

Fisher-Blando, J. L. (2008). Workplace bullying: Aggressive behavior and its effect on job satisfaction and productivity. Available from ProQuest Dissertations and Theses database. (UMI No. 3309257)

Forni, P. M. (2008). The civility solution: What to do when people are rude. New York, NY: St. Martin's Press.

Gardner, G. B. (2012). Mobbing: A not so new phenomenon. (Order No. 3572890, University of Phoenix). ProQuest Dissertations and Theses, , 354. Retrieved from http://search.proquest.com/docview/1433075032?accountid=35812. (1433075032).

Gibson, C. B., Porath, C. L., Benson, G. S., & Lawler, E. E. (2007). What results when firms implement practices: The differentia relationship between specific practices, firm financial performance, customer service, and quality? Journal of Applied Psychology, 92(6), 1467-1480. doi:10. 1037/0021-9010. 92. 6. 1467

Gill, M. J. (2007). The relative predictability of incivility on interpersonal and organizational trust. Available from ProQuest Dissertations and Theses database. (UMI No. 3291123)

Girardi, P., Monaco, E., Prestigiacomo, C., Talamo, A., Ruberto, A., & Tatarelli, R. (2007). Personality and psychopathological profiles in individuals exposed to mobbing. Violence & Victims, 22(2), 172-188. doi:10. 1891/088667007780477320

Goh, A. (2007). An attributional analysis of counterproductive work behavior (CWB) in response to occupational stress. Available from ProQuest Dissertations and Theses database. (UMI No. 3260059)

Goleman, D. (1996) Emotional Intelligence: Why it Can Matter More Than IQ

Goldsmith, M. (with Reiter, M.) (2007). What got you here did not get you there. New York, NY: Hyperion.

Gonthier, G. (with Morrissey, K.) (2002). Rude awakenings: Overcoming the civility crisis in the workplace. Chicago, IL: Dearborne Trade Publishing.

Grunau, G. (2007). Mobbing and burnout: Are they linked? (Order No. 3274555, Walden University). ProQuest Dissertations and Theses, , 129-n/a. Retrieved from http://search.proquest.com/docview/304769447?accountid=35812. (304769447).

Guinness, O. (2008). The case for civility: And why our future depends on it. New York, NY: HarperCollins.

Hames, M.E. (2013) Ethical Leadership As An Enabler Of Organizational Culture Change. Available from ProQuest Dissertations and Theses database UMI 3567265

Hemmings, p. A. (2013). Workplace Harassment And Bullying: U.S. Federal Employees. Available from ProQuest Dissertations and Theses database. (UMI 3588069)

Henderson, B. M. (2013). Workplace bullying: Applying Novak's (1998) learning theory to reducing manager bullying behavior. (Order No. 3554836, Capella University). ProQuest Dissertations and Theses, , 126. Retrieved from http://search.proquest.com/docview/1317633481?accountid=35812. (1317633481).

Hershcovis, M. S. (2006). The prediction and consequences of workplace aggression: A meta-analytic approach. (Order No. NR18518, Queen's University (Canada)). ProQuest Dissertations and Theses, , 183-183 p. Retrieved from http://search.proquest.com/docview/304971822? accountid=35812. (304971822).

Hintz Klein, A. M. (2012). Does workplace bullying matter? A descriptive study of the lived experience of the female professional target. (Order No. 3518067, Capella University). ProQuest Dissertations and Theses, , 206. Retrieved from http://search.proquest.com/docview/1033214198? accountid=35812. (1033214198).

Hutton, S. A. (2008). A longitudinal study of workplace incivility in a hospital. Available from ProQuest Dissertations and Theses database. (UMI No. 3323915)

Hwang, H. (2008). Why does incivility matter when communicating disagreement? Examining the psychological process of antagonism in political discussion. Available from ProQuest Dissertations and Theses database. (UMI No. 3327818)

Jacobs, H. (2013). An Examination Of Psychological Meaningfulness, Safety, And Availability As The Underlying Mechanisms Linking Job Features And Personal Characteristics To Work Engagement. Available from ProQuest Dissertations and Theses database. UMI Number: 3598079

James, D. M. (2013). Employee interpersonal communication: The relationship to morale within the professional learning community. (Order No. 3565659, Trevecca Nazarene University). ProQuest Dissertations and Theses, , 366. Retrieved from http://search.proquest.com/docview/1413324996? accountid=35812. (1413324996).

Jeter, S. J. (2010). Sabotage and workplace bullying: The bad and ugly of horizontal violence. (Order No. 1491103, Gardner-Webb University). ProQuest Dissertations and Theses, , 56. Retrieved from http://search.proquest.com/docview/864567194?accountid=35812. (864567194).

Johnson, J. E. (2008). Do parents try to bully teachers through confrontation? (Order No. DP19314, Virginia Polytechnic Institute and State University). ProQuest Dissertations and Theses, , 139. Retrieved from http://search.proquest.com/docview/1027590525?accountid=35812. (1027590525).

Johnson, S. L. (2013). An exploration of discourses of workplace bullying of organizations, regulatory agencies and hospital nursing unit managers. (Order No. 3588730, University of Washington). ProQuest Dissertations and Theses, , 174. Retrieved from http://search.proquest.com/docview/1428354694?accountid=35812. (1428354694).

Johnston, S. M. (2010). Reacting to abusive managerial behavior: A qualitative phenomenological study. Available from ProQuest Dissertations and Theses database. (UMI No. 3415970)

Kahn, W.A. (1990). Psychological Conditions of personal engagement and disengagement at work. Academy of Management Journal,

Kaster, J. T. (2004). Bystanding behavior in bullying situations among Icelandic adolescents: A qualitative and quantitative investigation. (Order No. 3156725, University of South Dakota). ProQuest Dissertations and Theses, , 30-30 p. Retrieved from http://search.proquest.com/docview/305117379?accountid=35812. (305117379).

Katcher, B. L. (with Snyder, A.) (2007). 30 reasons employees hate their managers. New York, NY: American Management Association.

Kelloway, K. E., Francis, L., Prosser, M., & Cameron, J. (2010). Counterproductive work behavior as protest. Human Resource Management Review, 20(1), 18-25. doi:10. 1016/j. hrmr. 2009. 03. 014

Kim, T. -Y., Shapiro, D. L., Aquino, K., Lim, V. K., & Bennett, R. J. (2008). Workplace offense and victims' reactions: The effects of victim-offender (dis)similarity, offense-type, and cultural differences. Journal of Organizational Behavior, 29(3), 415-433. doi:10. 1002/job. 519

Kokubun, S. (2007). Abusive behavior at work: A cross-cultural comparison between the united states and japan. (Order No. 3273300, Alliant International University, San Diego). ProQuest Dissertations and Theses, , 179. Retrieved from http://search.proquest.com/docview/304701815?accountid=35812. (304701815).

Kolbeck, D. (2013). Workplace bullying: Trauma spectrum symptoms in a community population of registered nurses. (Order No. 3559697, Alliant International University). ProQuest Dissertations and Theses, , 174. Retrieved from http://search.proquest.com/docview/1354430771?accountid=35812. (1354430771).

Kramen, A. J. (2002). Emotional regulation and emotional abuse: Can an abusive workplace be avoided? (Order No. 3060644, The University of Akron). ProQuest Dissertations and Theses, , 184-184 p. Retrieved from http://search.proquest.com/docview/304802379?accountid=35812. (304802379).

Lane, A. L. (2013). Antecedents to mobbing. (Order No. 1537662, Marshall University). ProQuest Dissertations and Theses, , 38. Retrieved from http://search.proquest.com/docview/1367082540?

accountid=35812. (1367082540).

Lawrence, T., & Robinson, S. (2007). Ain't misbehaving: Workplace deviance as organizational resistance. Journal of Management, 33(3), 378-394. doi:10. 1177/0149206307300816

Levine, E. L. (2010). Emotion and power (as social influence). Their effect on organizational citizenship and counterproductive individual and organizational behavior. Human Resource Management Review, 20(1), 4-17. doi:10. 1016/j. hrmr. 2009. 03. 011

Lewis, P. S. (2009). Individual and organizational factors that predict workplace incivility: Impact on costs, absenteeism, and productivity. Available from ProQuest Dissertations and Theses database. (UMI No. 3399054)

Lim, S., Cortina, L. M., & Magley, V. J. (2008). Personal and workgroup incivility: Effect on work and health outcomes. Journal of Applied Psychology, 93(1), 95-107. doi:10. 1037/0021-9010. 93. 1. 95

Lin, Y. (2007). Understanding school bullying and workplace abuse in a taiwanese context. (Order No. 3286046, Oregon State University). ProQuest Dissertations and Theses, , 221. Retrieved from http://search.proquest.com/docview/304820321?accountid=35812. (304820321).

Linvill, J. S. (2008). Surviving workplace incivility: the use of supportive networks as a coping strategy. Available from ProQuest Dissertations and Theses database. (UMI No. 1469706)

Liu, S. L. (2012). U.S. women bullying women in the pharmaceutical/biotechnology/medical device industry. (Order No. 3518867, Pepperdine University). ProQuest Dissertations and Theses, , 202. Retrieved from http://search.proquest.com/docview/1034289193?accountid=35812. (1034289193).

Liu, W., Chi, S. C., Friedman, R., & Tsai, M. H. (2009). Explaining incivility in the workplace: The effects of personality and culture. Negotiation and Conflict Management Research, 2(2), 164-184. doi:10. 1111/j. 1750-4716. 2009. 00035. x.

Lyons, B. (2010). Observer responses to workplace bullying: The dynamic influence of race and relational demography. (Order No. 1483484, Michigan State University). ProQuest Dissertations and Theses, , 90. Retrieved from http://search.proquest.com/docview/822764235?accountid=35812. (822764235).

MacLane, C. N., & Walmsley, P. T. (2010). Reducing counterproductive work behavior through employee selection. Human Resource Management Review, 20(1), 62-77. doi:10. 1016/j. hrmr. 2009. 05. 001

Marcello, C. V. (2010). A correlational analysis: Perceptions of workplace bullying and psychological empowerment among IT professionals. (Order No. 3411119, University of Phoenix). ProQuest Dissertations and Theses, , 222-n/a. Retrieved from http://search.proquest.com/docview/520405286?accountid=35812. (520405286).

Marchand-Stenhoff, S. M. (2009). Academic incivility in higher education. Available from ProQuest Dissertations and Theses database. (UMI No. 3386703)

Martin, R. J., & Hine, D. W. (2005). Development and validation of the uncivil workplace behavior questionnaire. Journal of Occupational Health Psychology, 10(4), 477-490. doi:10. 1037/1076-8998. 10. 4. 477

McKinne, M. (2008). A quantitative and qualitative inquiry into classroom incivility in higher education. Available from ProQuest Dissertations and Theses database. (UMI No. 3371082)

Meglich-Sespico, P. (2006). Perceived severity of interpersonal workplace harassment behaviors. (Order No. 3237843, Kent State University). ProQuest Dissertations and Theses, , 174-174 p. Retrieved from http://search.proquest.com/docview/305316660?accountid=35812. (305316660).

Milam, A. C., Spitzmueller, C., & Penney, L. M. (2009). Investigating individual differences among targets of workplace incivility. Journal of Occupational Health Psychology, 14(1), 58-69. doi:10. 1037/a0012683

Miner-Rubino, K. M., & Cortina, L. M. (2007). Beyond targets: Consequences of vicarious exposure to misogyny at work. Journal of Applied Psychology, 92(5), 1254-1269. doi:10. 1037/0021-9010. 92. 5. 1254

Mole, N. J. (2007). Protection and precariousness: Workplace mobbing, gender and neoliberalism in northern italy. (Order No. 3319442, Rutgers The State University of New Jersey - New Brunswick). ProQuest Dissertations and Theses, , 430. Retrieved from http://search.proquest.com/docview/304818109?accountid=35812. (304818109).

Morse, B. J., & Popovich, P. M. (2009). Realistic recruitment practices in organizations: The potential benefits of generalized expectancy calibration. Human Resource Management Review, 19(1), 1-8. doi:10. 1016/j. hrmr. 2008. 09. 002

Namie, G. (2003). Workplace bullying: Escalated incivility. Ivey Business Journal.

Namie, G. (2007). The challenge of workplace bullying. Employee Relations Today, 34, 2

Namie, G., & Namie, R. (2003). The bully at work: What you can do to stop the hurt and reclaim your dignity on the job. Naperville, IL: Source Books.

Nicol, J. E. (2006). The utility of self-labelling in the psychological and organisational outcomes of workplace bullying in a canadian student sample. (Order No. MR19115, University of Calgary (Canada)). ProQuest Dissertations and Theses, , 238-238 p. Retrieved from http://search.proquest.com/docview/305347058?accountid=35812. (305347058).

Nish, M. A. (2011). Realigning: A grounded theory of academic workplace conflict. (Order No. 3454329, Fielding Graduate University). ProQuest Dissertations and Theses, , 153. Retrieved from http://search.proquest.com/docview/868859178?accountid=35812. (868859178).

Nyborg, D. G. (2012). Sabotaging our sisters: Perceptions of female relational aggression in higher education among female faculty and administrators at three western U.S. universities. (Order No. 3536199, Idaho State University). ProQuest Dissertations and Theses, , 235. Retrieved from http://search.proquest.com/docview/1292616220?accountid=35812. (1292616220).

O'Donnell, S. M. (2009). Sickness absence among women who have experienced workplace bullying: A grounded theory study. (Order No. MR74330, University of New Brunswick (Canada)). ProQuest Dissertations and Theses, , 118. Retrieved from http://search.proquest.com/docview/872076726?accountid=35812. (872076726).

Olender-Russo, L. (2009). Creating a culture of regard: An antidote for workplace bullying. Creative Nursing, 15(2), 75-81. doi:10. 1891/1078-4535. 15. 2. 75

Olson, T. L. (2008). Do unto others as they would have you do, or business as usual? A study of workplace bullying in California central valley K--6 schools. (Order No. 3338010, University of La Verne). ProQuest Dissertations and Theses, , 242. Retrieved from http://search.proquest.com/docview/304376325?accountid=35812. (304376325).

Osatuke, K., Moore, S. C., Ward, C., Dryenforth, S. R., & Belton, L. (2009). Civility, respect, engagement in the workforce (CREW); Nationwide organization development intervention at Veterans Health Administration. The Journal of Applied Behavioral Science, 45(3), 384-410. doi:10. 1177/0021886309335067

Out, J. W. (2005). Meanings of workplace bullying: Labelling versus experiencing and the belief in a just world. (Order No. NR09718, University of Windsor (Canada)). ProQuest Dissertations and Theses, , 187-187 p. Retrieved from http://search.proquest.com/docview/304990680?accountid=35812. (304990680).

Palmer, R. R., & Colton, J. (1995). A history of the modern world (8th ed.). New York, NY: McGraw Hill.

Patterson, K. E. (2011). The occurrence and outcome of workplace bullying among emerging adults. (Order No. MR81601, Carleton University (Canada)). ProQuest Dissertations and Theses, , 163. Retrieved from http://search.proquest.com/docview/916257373?accountid=35812. (916257373).

Pearson, C. M., & Porath, C. L. (2005). On the nature, consequences, and remedies of workplace incivility: No time for "nice"? Think again. Academy of Management Executive, 19(1), 7-18. doi:10. 5465/AME. 2005. 15841946

Pearson, C. M., & Porath, C. L. (2009). The cost of bad behavior. New York, NY: The Penguin Group.

Pearson, C. M., & Porath, C. L. (2010). Zero tolerance: Business leaders who understand the cost of incivility in their organizations make eliminating bad behavior a priority. American Executive, 8(5), 14-16. Retrieved from http://www. americanexecutive. com/departments/best-practices/7557-best-practices-zero-tolerance

Pearson, C. M., Andersson, L. M., & Porath, C. L. (2000). Assessing and attacking and workplace incivility. Organizational Dynamics, 29(2), 123-137. doi:10. 1016/S0090-2616(00)00019-X

Pearson, C. M., Andersson, L., & Wegner, J. (2001). When workers flout convention: A study of workplace incivility. Human Relations, 54(1), 1387-1419. doi:10. 1177/00187267015411001.

Penney, L. M. (2006). Workplace incivility. In S. G. Rogelberg (Ed.), Encyclopedia of industrial and organizational psychology (Vol. 2, p. 896-897). Thousand Oaks, CA: Sage Publications. Retrieved from http://www. sage-ereference. com/organizationalpsychology/Article_n375. html

Penttila, C. (2009). Employees, leave the attitude at the door. Entrepreneur, 37(4), 60. Retrieved from http://www. entrepreneur. com/magazine/entrepreneur/2009/april/200748. html

Pepperdine University Graduate School of Education and Psychology

Phillips, T., & Smith, P. (2004). Emotional and behavioral responses to everyday incivility: Challenging the fear/avoidance paradigm. Journal of Sociology, 40(4), 378-399. doi:10. 1177/1440783304048382

Plavinskis, S. (2006). Guerrillas in the mi(d)st: A study of discreet dissension among administrators in academe. (Order No. MR24514, Brock University (Canada)). ProQuest Dissertations and Theses, , 103-103 p. Retrieved from http://search.proquest.com/docview/304914084?accountid=35812. (304914084).

Popovich, P. M., & Warren, M. A. (2010). The role of power in sexual harassment as a counterproductive behavior in organizations. Human Resource Management Review, 20(1), 45-53. doi:10. 1016/j. hrmr. 2009. 05. 003

Porath, C. L., & Erez, A. (2007). Does rudeness really matter? The effects of rudeness on task performance and helpfulness. Academy of Management Journal, 50(5), 1181-1197. doi:10. 2307/20159919

Powell, A. L. (2012). The effects of workplace incivility, workplace bullying, and school culture on student achievement. (Order No. 3531431, University of Louisville). ProQuest Dissertations and Theses, , 155. Retrieved from http://search.proquest.com/docview/1151691603?accountid=35812. (1151691603).

Reio, T. J., & Ghosh, R. (2009). Antecedents and outcomes of workplace incivility: Implications for human resource development research and practice. Human Resource Development Quarterly, 20(3), 237-264. doi:10. 1002/hrdq. 20020

Roberts, S. J. (2009). Incivility as a function of workplace favoritism and employee impulsivity. Available from ProQuest Dissertations and Theses database. (UMI No. 1462135)

Robertson, T. E. (2011). A complex and dangerous world: Two sets of evidence for the recalibrational theory of exclusion response. (Order No. 3473789, University of California, Santa Barbara). ProQuest Dissertations and Theses, , 196. Retrieved from http://search.proquest.com/docview/896615854?accountid=35812. (896615854).

Roscigno, V. J., Hodson, R., & Lopez, S. H. (2009). Workplace incivilities: The role of interest conflicts, social closure, and organizational chaos. Work, Employment & Society, 23(4), 747-773. doi:10. 1177/0950017009344875

Rosette, C. L. (2013). A qualitative inquiry of professional women who have experienced isolation as a form of bullying in the workplace. (Order No. 3562382, Capella University). ProQuest Dissertations and Theses, , 135. Retrieved from http://search.proquest.com/docview/1369844493?accountid=35812. (1369844493).

Rouse, L. (2013). The impact of workplace bullying on health care workers. (Order No. 3603830, Walden University). ProQuest Dissertations and Theses, , 133. Retrieved from http://search.proquest.com/docview/1473904453?accountid=35812. (1473904453).

Santos, S. (2014). Beauvoirian therapy: Treating depression arising from oppressive conditions via Beauvoirian ethics. (Order No. NS28278, University of Manitoba (Canada)). ProQuest Dissertations and Theses, , 193. Retrieved from http://search.proquest.com/docview/1516520079?accountid=35812. (1516520079).

Sartain, S. S. (2013). Workplace bullying: Protective mechanisms between bullying and post-traumatic stress disorder. (Order No. 3589460, Capella University). ProQuest Dissertations and Theses, , 140. Retrieved from http://search.proquest.com/docview/1430559715?accountid=35812. (1430559715).

Sauer, P. A. (2013). Does resilience mediate the effects of bullying in nurses? (Order No. 3568910, The University of North Carolina at Greensboro). ProQuest Dissertations and Theses, , 169. Retrieved from http://search.proquest.com/docview/1426828537?accountid=35812. (1426828537).

Schat, A. C. H. (2004). In praise of intolerance: Investigating the effects of organizational tolerance on the incidence and consequences of workplace aggression. (Order No. NQ94993, University of Guelph (Canada)). ProQuest Dissertations and Theses, , 224-224 p. Retrieved from http://search.proquest.com/docview/305190335?accountid=35812. (305190335).

Sharifi, J. (2012). Violence at work: Labeling aggressive behavior as bullying. (Order No. 3506850, TUI University). ProQuest Dissertations and Theses, , 276. Retrieved from http://search.proquest.com/docview/1011645154?accountid=35812. (1011645154).

Sharon, S. (2010). Abusive behavior in organizations: A cross-cultural comparison between the U.S. and Israel. (Order No. 3451862, Alliant International University, San Diego). ProQuest Dissertations and Theses, , 133. Retrieved from http://search.proquest.com/docview/863204281?accountid=35812. (863204281).

Shorenstein, A. (2007). Bearing witness: Workplace mobbing and the observer's quandary. (Order No. 3268624, The Wright Institute). ProQuest Dissertations and Theses, , 91-n/a. Retrieved from http://search.proquest.com/docview/304809419?accountid=35812. (304809419).

Simmons, D. C. (2008). Organizational culture, workplace incivility, and turnover: The impact of human resources practices. Available from ProQuest Dissertations and Theses database. (UMI No. 3308361)

Skorek, J. L. (2009). A qualitative study of counseling interventions used to assist targets of workplace bullying. (Order No. 3359038, Northern Illinois University). ProQuest Dissertations and

Theses, , 258. Retrieved from http://search.proquest.com/docview/304968730?accountid=35812. (304968730).

Smith, P., Phillips, T. L., & King, R. D. (2010). Incivility: The rude stranger in everyday life. New York, NY: Cambridge University Press.

Steinhauser, E. F. (2012). Psychological bullying climate: Measurement development and validation. (Order No. 3529204, Florida Institute of Technology). ProQuest Dissertations and Theses, , 298. Retrieved from http://search.proquest.com/docview/1095739358?accountid=35812. (1095739358).

St-Pierre, I. (2010). Understanding the management of Intra/Inter professional aggression: A critical nursing ethnography. (Order No. NR73915, University of Ottawa (Canada)). ProQuest Dissertations and Theses, , 305. Retrieved from http://search.proquest.com/docview/870516184?accountid=35812. (870516184).

Sutton, R. I. (2010). The no asshole rule: Building a civilized workplace and surviving one that isn't. New York, NY: The Hatchet Book Group.

Sweeney, J. (2007). Return to civility. Minneapolis, MN: Aerialist Press.

Tagle, M. P. (2009). Narrativizing Chilean nurses' accounts of workplace bullying: Communicative processes of mystification, constrained and contested agency. (Order No. 3379772, Purdue University). ProQuest Dissertations and Theses, , 243. Retrieved from http://search.proquest.com/docview/304990716?accountid=35812. (304990716).

Taylor, S. G. (2010). Cold looks and hot tempers: individual-level effects of incivility in the workplace (Unpublished doctoral dissertation). Louisiana State University, Louisiana.

Thau, S., Aquino, K., & Wittek, R. (2007). An extension of uncertainty management theory to the self: The relationship between justice, social comparison orientation, and antisocial work behaviors. Journal of Applied Psychology, 92(1), 250-258. doi:10. 1037/0021-9010. 92. 1. 250

Threadgill, C. R. (2013). Perceptions of workplace bullying among practicing registered nurses. (Order No. 3569775, The University of Southern Mississippi). ProQuest Dissertations and Theses, , 216. Retrieved from http://search.proquest.com/docview/1371926887?accountid=35812. (1371926887).

Tiller, V. T. (2010). Depression in middle managers who are targets of workplace bullying. (Order No. 3396811, Walden University). ProQuest Dissertations and Theses, , 142. Retrieved from http://search.proquest.com/docview/193269441?accountid=35812. (193269441).

Trudel, J. (2009). Workplace incivility: Relationship with conflict management styles and impact on perceived job performance, organizational commitment, and turnover. Available from ProQuest Dissertations and Theses database. (UMI No. 3381935)

Tunajek, S. (2007). Workplace incivility - Part I: Anger, harassment, and horizontal violence. AANA Journal, 61(3), 30-31. http://search. proquest. com. ezproxy. apollolibrary. com/docview/222281210?accountid=35812

Turnage, A. K. (2008). Email flaming behaviors and organizational conflict. Journal of Computer Mediated Communication, 13(1), 43-59. doi:10. 1111/J. 1083-6101. 2007. 00385. x

Vandenberg, M. (2012). Bullying in small town service providers in northern British Columbia: The experience of executive directors and putting theory into practice. (Order No. MR87543, University of Northern British Columbia (Canada)). ProQuest Dissertations and Theses, , 96. Retrieved from http://search.proquest.com/docview/1026830404?accountid=35812. (1026830404).

Vickers, M. (2006). Writing what's relevant: Workplace incivility in public administration—A wolf in sheep's clothing. Administrative Theory and Praxis,

Vickers, M. H. (2006). Writing what's relevant: Workplace incivility in public administration-a wolf in sheep's clothing. Administrative Theory & Praxis, 28(1), 69-88. Retrieved from http://search. proquest. com. ezproxy. apollolibrary. com/docview/196609407?accountid=35812

Wachs, J. (2009). Workplace incivility, bullying, and mobbing. AAOHN Journal, 57(2), 88. Retrieved from http://search. proquest. com. ezproxy. apollolibrary. com/docview/219401239? accountid=35812

Wagner, K. D. (2000). Simulation models of evolution: Communication and cooperation. (Order No. 9981093, Indiana University). ProQuest Dissertations and Theses, , 170-170 p. Retrieved from http://search.proquest.com/docview/304596503?accountid=35812. (304596503).

Walter, F., & Bruch, H. (2008). The positive group affect spiral: A dynamic model of the emergence of positive affective similarity in work groups. Journal of Organizational Behavior, 29(2), 239-261. doi:10. 1002/job. 505

Wardell, M. M. (2011). The effects of bullying on men and women in American workplaces. (Order No. 3482735, Walden University). ProQuest Dissertations and Theses, , 127. Retrieved from http://search.proquest.com/docview/910844170?accountid=35812. (910844170).

Wikipedia. (2014)http://en.wikipedia.org/wiki/Dragon%27s_teeth_(mythology).

Wilkin, L. V. (2010). Workplace Bullying in Academe: A Grounded Theory Study Exploring How Faculty Cope With the Experience of Being Bullied. Available from ProQuest Dissertations and Theses database. (UMI No. 3447190)

Wilson, T. A. (2010). Workplace aggression behaviors, organizational justice, and intention to leave among U.S. telecommunications workers. (Order No. 3406165, Lynn University). ProQuest Dissertations and Theses, , 366-n/a. Retrieved from http://search.proquest.com/docview/275596271? accountid=35812. (275596271).

Wood, J. D., I.I.I. (2008). Bullying cognitions through identification with fictional characters. (Order No. 3328244, George Fox University). ProQuest Dissertations and Theses, , 40. Retrieved from http://search.proquest.com/docview/304808882?accountid=35812. (304808882).

Yeung, A., & Griffin, B. (2008). Workplace incivility: Does it matter in Asia? People and Strategy, 31(3), 14-19. Retrieved from http://search. proquest. com. ezproxy. apollolibrary.

com/docview/224579754?accountid=35812

Zippel, K. S. (2000). Policies against sexual harassment: Gender equality policies in Germany, the European union, and the united states in comparative perspective. (Order No. 9982234, The University of Wisconsin - Madison). ProQuest Dissertations and Theses, , 399-399 p. Retrieved from http://search.proquest.com/docview/304636470?accountid=35812. (304636470).